Coding Guidelines for React with TypeScript

Iulian Radu

Independently published
Paperback ISBN: 9798335831383

In **Coding Guidelines for React with TypeScript**, you'll discover a comprehensive collection of best practices and principles honed through over 25 years of software development experience and more than a decade of building web applications using React and TypeScript. This book is designed to help developers at all levels write clean, maintainable, and efficient code in modern JavaScript frameworks.

Programming with React and TypeScript by using Clean Code rules provides a comprehensive design for developers who seek to build scalable, maintainable, and robust applications by writing code that is not only functional but also readable, modular, and easy to maintain.

Whether you're a seasoned professional or just starting out, this book provides clear and actionable guidelines to improve your code quality. You'll learn how to structure your projects, manage state effectively, and create reusable components that adhere to the principles of clean code. The book covers crucial topics such as file organization, the importance of meaningful naming, avoiding common pitfalls like excessive `if-else` statements, and the benefits of early returns in functions.

Additionally, you'll explore advanced topics like state management with Redux Toolkit, the separation of concerns, and how to maximize code coverage through strategic testing practices. Each guideline is backed by practical examples and explanations that illustrate why these practices matter in real-world development.

Coding Guidelines for React with TypeScript is not just a set of rules; it's a roadmap to writing better code, informed by decades of hands-on experience. Whether you're working on a small project or a large-scale application, these guidelines will help you build robust, scalable, and maintainable software.

Understanding the Web Applications

Web applications are interactive programs that run on web servers and are accessed by users through web browsers over the Internet or an Intranet. Unlike traditional desktop applications, web applications do not need to be installed on the user's device; they are accessible via a URL.

Key Characteristics of Web Applications

- Accessibility
Accessible from any device with a web browser and an Internet connection.

- Interactivity
Provide a rich, interactive user experience, often similar to desktop applications.

- Centralized Updates
Updates are applied centrally on the server, so all users have access to the latest version without needing to install updates manually.

- Cross-Platform
Can be used across various operating systems and devices.

What is a Web Server?

A web server is a software or hardware system that serves web content to clients over the internet or intranet. It handles requests from clients (usually web browsers) and responds by sending the requested resources such as HTML pages, images, videos, and other files. It also processes and serves dynamic content generated by server-side scripts and applications.

Key Functions of a Web Server

● Handling Requests
Receives HTTP requests from clients and processes them.

● Serving Static Content
Delivers static files (e.g., HTML, CSS, JavaScript, images) to clients.

● Executing Server-Side Code
Processes server-side scripts (e.g., PHP, Python) and generates dynamic content.

● Managing Sessions
Handles user sessions and cookies for state management.

● Logging and Monitoring
Logs server activity and provides monitoring capabilities

for performance and security.

Most Used Web Server Software

● Apache HTTP Server
Often referred to as Apache, it is one of the oldest and most widely used web servers.

● Nginx
Nginx is known for its high performance, scalability, and low resource consumption.

● Microsoft Internet Information Services (IIS)
IIS is a web server developed by Microsoft for Windows Server.

● Tomcat
Apache Tomcat is a web server and servlet container for Java applications.

What is a Web Browser?

A web browser is a software application used to access, retrieve, and display content from the web. It interprets and renders HTML (HyperText Markup Language), CSS (Cascading Style Sheets), and JavaScript to present web pages to users. Browsers also handle various types of web content, such as images, videos, and interactive elements.

Key Functions of a Web Browser

- **Request and Retrieval**
Sends requests to web servers for content and retrieves the data.

- **Rendering**
Interprets HTML, CSS, and JavaScript to display web pages.

- **Navigation**
Allows users to navigate between web pages using URLs (Uniform Resource Locators).

- **Bookmarking**
Enables users to save and organize links to frequently visited sites.

● Security
Provides features like encryption (HTTPS), private browsing, and protection against malicious sites.

● Extensions/Add-ons
Supports extensions and plugins to enhance functionality, such as ad-blockers or password managers.

Most Used Web Browsing Engines

The web rendering engine is a crucial component of a web browser responsible for interpreting and displaying web content. Different browsers use different engines, each with its own strengths and features. Here are the most commonly used web rendering engines:

● Blink
Blink is the rendering engine used by Google Chrome, Microsoft Edge (Chromium-based), and other browsers built on the Chromium platform.

● WebKit
WebKit is the rendering engine used by Apple Safari and some other browsers.

● Gecko
Gecko is the rendering engine used by Mozilla Firefox.

Understanding these engines helps developers ensure that their web applications work consistently across different browsers and platforms by accounting for differences in rendering behavior and support for web standards.

What is the Web Page Structure?

The web page structure refers to the organization and arrangement of elements within a web page. It encompasses how different components like content, images, and interactive elements are laid out and structured in relation to each other. This structure is defined using HTML (HyperText Markup Language) and styled with CSS (Cascading Style Sheets).

A well-structured web page ensures that content is presented in a logical, accessible, and user-friendly manner. It also facilitates better performance, easier maintenance, and improved search engine optimization (SEO).

HTML Document Structure

- Doctype Declaration
Specifies the HTML version and helps browsers render the page correctly.

- <html> Element
The root element that contains all other elements on the page.

- \<head\> Element

Contains meta-information about the page, including:

Metadata

Information about the page (e.g., charset, viewport settings).

Title

The title of the page, displayed in the browser tab.

Links to CSS

Stylesheets that define the pages appearance.

Scripts

JavaScript files or inline scripts.

- \<body\> Element

Contains the content of the page that is visible to users, including:

Header

Typically includes navigation and introductory content.

Main Content

The primary content of the page.

Footer

Contains supplementary information like copyright

notices and additional links.

HTML Elements and Their Roles

Document Structure Elements:

<!DOCTYPE html>: Declares the document type and version of HTML.
<html>: Root element of the HTML document.
<head>: Contains meta-information about the document.
<title>: Defines the title of the document (displayed in the browsers title bar).
<meta>: Provides metadata about the HTML document (e.g., charset, viewport settings).
<link>: Links to external resources like stylesheets.
<style>: Contains internal CSS styles.
<script>: Includes or links to JavaScript files or scripts.
<body>: Contains the content of the document that is visible to users.

Text Content Elements:

- Headings: Define the structure of the document.
  <h1> to <h6>: Define headings of different levels.
- Paragraphs: Define blocks of text.
  <p>: Represents a paragraph.
- Line Breaks and Horizontal Rules:

: Inserts a line break.
  <hr>: Creates a horizontal rule (line).

Grouping Content:

- Sections: Group content into logical sections.
  <section>: Represents a generic section of content.
  <article>: Represents a self-contained piece of content.
  <aside>: Represents content indirectly related to the main content.
  <nav>: Defines navigation links.
  <header>: Represents introductory content or a set of navigational links.
  <footer>: Represents footer content, typically for the entire document or a section.
  <div>: Generic container for grouping and styling content.
  <span>: Generic inline container for styling and grouping small pieces of content.
- Unordered Lists: Create lists with bullet points.
  <ul>: Defines an unordered list.
  <li>: Defines a list item within <ul>.
- Ordered Lists: Create lists with numbered items.
  <ol>: Defines an ordered list.
  <li>: Defines a list item within <ol>.
- Definition Lists: Create lists of terms and definitions.
  <dl>: Defines a definition list.
  <dt>: Defines a term in a definition list.
  <dd>: Defines a description or definition of a term.

Tables:

- Table Structure: Create tabular data.
  <table>: Defines a table.
  <caption>: Provides a caption for the table.
  <thead>: Groups the header content in a table.
  <tbody>: Groups the body content in a table.
  <tfoot>: Groups the footer content in a table.
  <tr>: Defines a row in a table.
  <th>: Defines a header cell in a table.
  <td>: Defines a standard cell in a table.

Forms and Input Elements:

- Form Container: Encloses form elements.
  <form>: Defines a form for user input.
- Input Fields: Collect user data.
  <input>: Defines an input field.
  <textarea>: Defines a multi-line text input field.
  <button>: Defines a clickable button.
  <select>: Defines a dropdown list.
  <option>: Defines an option in a dropdown list.
  <label>: Defines a label for an <input> element.
  <fieldset>: Groups related elements in a form.
  <legend>: Provides a caption for a <fieldset>.

Embedded Content:

- Images and Media: Embed images, audio, and video.
  <img>: Embeds an image.
  <audio>: Defines sound content.
  <video>: Defines video content.
  <source>: Defines multiple media resources for <audio> and <video>.
  <track>: Provides text tracks for <video> and <audio>.
- Iframes: Embed another HTML document.
  <iframe>: Defines an inline frame.

Links and Anchors:

- Hyperlinks: Create links to other resources.
  <a>: Defines a hyperlink.
- Anchor Links: Create links to specific parts of the same document.
  <a href="#sectionId">: Link to an element with a specific id.

Scripting:

- JavaScript Integration: Include or link to JavaScript code.
  <script>: Defines a client-side script.

Meta Information:

● Metadata: Provide additional information about the document.
  <meta>: Defines metadata such as character set, author, and viewport settings.

Understanding these categories helps in effectively using HTML to build and style web content. This structure is fundamental to web development, ensuring that content is presented clearly and effectively to users.

What is the DOM?

The Document Object Model (DOM) is a programming interface for web documents. It represents the page so that programs can change the document structure, style, and content. The DOM is an object-oriented representation of the web page, which can be modified with a scripting language such as JavaScript.

Key Features of the DOM

• Tree Structure
The DOM represents a document as a tree of nodes, where each node is an object representing part of the document. Nodes can be elements, attributes, text, and more.

• Dynamic Manipulation
You can use JavaScript to dynamically manipulate the content and structure of the document. This includes adding, removing, and modifying elements and attributes.

• Event Handling
The DOM allows you to attach event listeners to elements, enabling interactive web applications. For example, you can listen for clicks, mouse movements, and other user actions.

- Cross-Platform

The DOM is a standard interface supported by all modern browsers, ensuring that web pages behave consistently across different environments.

What is the Shadow DOM?

The Shadow DOM is a part of the Web Components specification. It allows for encapsulation of DOM and CSS, providing a way to isolate styles and scripts within a component, preventing them from affecting the rest of the document.

Key Features of the Shadow DOM

- Encapsulation

The Shadow DOM allows you to encapsulate the internal structure and style of a web component, keeping it separate from the main DOM.

- Scoped Styling

Styles defined within a shadow DOM are scoped to that particular shadow tree and do not affect the main document or other shadow trees.

- Reusable Components

Shadow DOM is commonly used in building reusable web components that work consistently across different parts of an application or even across different applications.

Differences Between DOM and Shadow DOM

- Encapsulation

DOM: No encapsulation; styles and scripts affect the entire document.

Shadow DOM: Encapsulated; styles and scripts within a shadow DOM do not affect the main document or other components.

- Usage

DOM: Used for the general structure and manipulation of web documents.

Shadow DOM: Used for creating isolated, reusable web components.

- Scoping

DOM: Styles and scripts are globally scoped.

Shadow DOM: Styles and scripts are scoped to the shadow DOM tree.

- Interoperability

DOM: All elements in the document are part of a single tree structure.

Shadow DOM: Each shadow root creates a separate tree within the main document tree.

By understanding both the DOM and the Shadow DOM, developers can create more modular, maintainable, and scalable web applications.

HTML Semantics and Its Use in React

HTML Semantics refers to the practice of using HTML elements that convey the meaning and structure of the content. Semantic HTML tags help both developers and browsers understand the purpose of the content within the tags, improving accessibility, SEO, and maintainability.

Benefits of Semantic HTML

- Accessibility
Semantic tags provide context to screen readers and assistive technologies, making web content more accessible to users with disabilities.

- SEO
Search engines use semantic HTML to better understand the content and structure of a webpage, which can improve search rankings.

- Maintainability
Code is more readable and easier to maintain when semantic tags are used, as they clearly describe the content and its role.

- Consistency
Using semantic tags promotes a consistent structure

across different pages and projects.

Common Semantic HTML Elements

<header> Represents the introductory content or a set of navigational links.
<nav> Contains navigation links.
<main> Denotes the main content of the document.
<section> Defines a section in a document.
<article> Represents a self-contained composition in a document.
<aside> Contains content that is tangentially related to the content around it.
<footer> Defines the footer for a section or document.
<h1> to <h6> Represent headings, with <h1> being the highest level.
<figure> Specifies content like illustrations, diagrams, or photos, along with their captions.
<figcaption> Provides a caption for a <figure> element.

Using Semantic HTML with React

In React, you can directly use semantic HTML tags within your components. Here is how to do it effectively:

• Use Semantic Tags in JSX
Replace generic <div> and <span> tags with semantic tags that describe the content more precisely.

- Component Organization

Organize your React components to reflect the semantic structure of the content.

- Accessibility Practices

Combine semantic HTML with ARIA (Accessible Rich Internet Applications) attributes to enhance accessibility further.

Example: Semantic HTML in a React Component

```
export function App() {
 return (
  <div>
   <header>
    <h1>My Website</h1>
    <nav>
     <ul>
      <li><a href="#home">Home</a></li>
      <li><a href="#about">About</a></li>
      <li><a href="#contact">Contact</a></li>
     </ul>
    </nav>
   </header>
   <main>
    <article>
     <h2>Article Title</h2>
     <p>This is an article about semantic HTML.</p>
    </article>
    <aside>
     <h3>Related Content</h3>
```

```
      <p>Here are some links to related content.</p>
      </aside>
    </main>
    <footer>
     <p>&copy; 2024 My Website</p>
    </footer>
  </div>
 );
};
```

In this example:

<header> element wraps the sites header, including the logo and navigation links.

<nav> element contains the navigation links.

<main> element encloses the primary content of the page.

<article> element represents an article section within the main content.

<aside> element contains related content or sidebars.

<footer> element defines the footer of the page.

Enhancing Accessibility with ARIA

While semantic HTML provides basic accessibility, sometimes you need additional ARIA attributes to fully support assistive technologies. For example:

```
export function App() {
 return (
  <div>
   <header role="banner">
    <h1>My Website</h1>
    <nav role="navigation" aria-label="Main navigation">
```

```
    <ul>
      <li><a href="#home">Home</a></li>
      <li><a href="#about">About</a></li>
      <li><a href="#contact">Contact</a></li>
    </ul>
   </nav>
  </header>
  <main role="main">
   <article>
    <h2>Article Title</h2>
    <p>This is an article about semantic HTML.</p>
   </article>
   <aside role="complementary">
    <h3>Related Content</h3>
    <p>Here are some links to related content.</p>
   </aside>
  </main>
  <footer role="contentinfo">
   <p>&copy; 2024 My Website</p>
  </footer>
 </div>
 );
};
```

Using semantic HTML in React enhances accessibility, SEO, and code maintainability. By incorporating semantic tags and ARIA attributes, you create a more structured, understandable, and user-friendly web application. This adherence to semantic principles aligns with clean code practices, resulting in a codebase that is not only functional but also robust and maintainable.

The Coding Guidelines for React with TypeScript

These principles and rules help developers write clean, maintainable, and readable code, leading to more robust and easier-to-maintain software systems.

Naming Conventions

Types should be named using PascalCase (capitalized words).

```
type UserProfile = {
  name: string;
  age: number;
  isActive: boolean;
};
```

Interfaces should be named using PascalCase, just like types.

```
interface User {
  id: number;
  profile: UserProfile;
}
```

Variables should be named using camelCase (lowercase first letter, with subsequent words capitalized). If possible, the boolean variables should start with "is".

```
const userName = 'JohnDoe';
let userAge = 25;
const isUserActive = true;
```

Functions should also be named using camelCase, similar to variables.

```
function getUserName(): string {
  return userName;
}
```

```
const calculateAge = (birthYear: number): number => {
  return new Date().getFullYear() - birthYear;
};
```

Use PascalCase to name your React components.

```
function UserProfile() {
  return <div>User Profile</div>;
}
```

Classes should be named using PascalCase too.

```
class UserManager {
  private users: User[] = [];
  addUser(user: User) {
    this.users.push(user);
  }
}
```

Enums should be named using PascalCase, while the values within the enum should be all uppercase, often separated by underscores.

```
enum UserRole {
  ADMIN = 'ADMIN',
  USER = 'USER',
  GUEST_USER = 'GUEST USER'
}
```

When naming functions, the scope and purpose of the function should guide the length and descriptiveness of its name. This rule helps make your code more readable and maintainable.

Use shorter, concise names for functions that have a narrow, localized scope, such as private methods, helper functions, or utility functions that are only used within a specific module or class. Since these functions are only relevant within a limited context, shorter names make the code easier to read without sacrificing clarity.

```
// Shorter name for a method with narrow scope
private log(msg: string): void {
  console.log(msg);
}
```

Use longer, more descriptive names for functions with a broader scope or that are publicly accessible, such as API methods, public class methods, or utility functions that are used across multiple modules. These functions are likely to be used or referenced in various parts of the codebase, so having a descriptive name helps communicate their purpose and usage to other developers.

```
// Longer, descriptive name for a function with broader
scope
function fetchUserDataById(userId: string):
Promise<UserData> {
  return apiClient.get(`/users/${userId}`);
}
function validateAndSaveUser(user: User): void {
  if (isValidUser(user)) {
    saveUserToDatabase(user);
  }
}
```

For React components, use **handle** as a prefix for internal event handler functions (those defined within the component), and use **on** for callback functions passed as props. This naming convention improves code readability by clearly distinguishing between locally defined handlers and those received from parent components. It also ensures consistency, making it easier to maintain and debug your code. For examples, use:

- handleClick for internal handlers.
- onClick for props passed into the component.

Using Meaningful Names

Using meaningful name is crucial for writing clean, maintainable, and understandable code. Meaningful names provide context and clarity, making it easier for developers to understand and work with the codebase. Here are the key benefits:

Meaningful names convey the purpose and usage of variables, functions, classes, and components. Other developers (or you in the future) can quickly understand what "userEmail" represents without needing additional comments or context.

```
// Good
const userEmail = "example@example.com";
// Bad
const u = "example@example.com";
```

Code with meaningful names often requires fewer comments, as the names themselves explain their purpose. Reduces the need for maintaining additional comments and helps avoid outdated or misleading documentation.

```
// Good
const isUserAuthenticated = true;
// Bad
const authFlag = true; // true if user is authenticated
```

Meaningful names make it easier for team members to communicate about the code. Team discussions and code reviews become more effective, as everyone can easily understand the function's purpose.

```
// Good
function calculateTotalPrice(items: Item[]): number {
  // ...
}
// Bad
function calc(items: Item[]): number {
  // ...
}
```

Descriptive names reduce the likelihood of misinterpretation and incorrect usage of variables and functions. Decreases the chance of using a variable incorrectly due to unclear or ambiguous names.

```
// Good
const userCount = 10;
// Bad
const count = 10;
```

Code with meaningful names is easier to refactor, as the purpose of each variable, function, and component is clear. Refactoring tools in IDEs can more accurately update code, and developers can more confidently make changes.

```
// Good
function sendEmail(to: string, subject: string, body: string): void {}
// Bad
function fn1(a: string, b: string, c: string): void {}
```

Using meaningful names encourages consistency in naming conventions across the codebase. Consistent naming conventions make the codebase easier to navigate and understand, especially in large projects.

```
// Good
interface User {
  firstName: string;
  lastName: string;
}
// Bad
interface U {
  fn: string;
  ln: string;
}
```

Meaningful names help identify issues more quickly during debugging. When inspecting variables during debugging, meaningful names provide immediate context, making it easier to locate and fix issues.

```
// Good
const activeUsers = getUsersByStatus("active");
// Bad
const x = getUsersByStatus("active");
```

Practical Tips for Using Meaningful Names

Use names that describe the data stored in the variable.

```
// Good
const userAge = 25;
// Bad
const age = 25;
```

Functions should be named based on the action they perform.

```
// Good
function fetchUserData()
// Bad
function getData()
```

React components should have names that reflect their purpose or what they render.

```
// Good
function UserProfile() {}
// Bad
function Profile() {}
```

Follow naming conventions: camelCase for variables and functions, PascalCase for classes and components.

```
// Good
const userAge = 25;
class UserProfile {}
```

Avoid short or ambiguous abbreviations that might be unclear or they can mislead readers.

```
// Good
const userEmail = "example@example.com";
let healthPoints: number = 120;
class ResourcesManager { }
// Bad
const ue = "example@example.com";
let hp: number = 120;   // "health points", "horsepower",
"hire purchase" ?
class Manager { }   // employees, resources, files,
```

Names should be distinct and avoid numeric suffixes or other disambiguation strategies.

```
// Good
const regularUser = "john";
const adminUser = "root";
// Bad
const user = "john";
const userAdmin = "root";
const user2 = "smith";
```

Use pronounceable names as it is easier to discuss and communicate.

Use searchable names to make it easier to find the code using search tools.

```
// Good
const roundButton = ...;
const linearProgressBar = ...;
// Bad
const round = ...;
const linear = ...;
```

Use consistent naming patterns across the codebase. For example, if you use fetch for data retrieval functions, stick to it (fetchUserData, fetchProductData).

Do not include type or scope information in names (e.g., Hungarian notation).

```
// Good
const maxUsers = 100;
const welcomeMessage = "Welcome!";
const isUserLoggedIn = false;
// Bad
const nMaxUsers = 100;
const sWelcomeMessage = "Welcome!";
const bIsUserLoggedIn = false;
```

By adhering to these practices, you ensure that your TypeScript code remains clean, understandable, and maintainable, leading to more efficient development and collaboration.

Shadowing Variable Names

Variable shadowing occurs when a variable declared within a certain scope (e.g., a function or a block) has the same name as a variable declared in an outer scope. This means that the inner variable "shadows" or "overrides" the outer variable within its scope. Avoid shadowing variable names in your code to prevent confusion, errors, and maintain code clarity.

Shadowing creates ambiguity about which variable is being referenced, especially in large functions or complex scopes. It makes the code harder to read and understand. The shadowed variable may lead to misleading context, where developers might incorrectly assume that they are referring to a variable with a broader scope.

Shadowing can lead to unintended behavior, as changes to the inner variable may affect the logic in unexpected ways. It can also cause bugs that are difficult to trace. Future modifications to the code can inadvertently affect the shadowed variable, introducing subtle bugs that are hard to identify and fix.

Shadowed variables increase code complexity, making it more challenging to maintain and extend. New developers or even the original author may struggle to keep track of variable usage. Refactoring code with shadowed variables can be more difficult, as you need to carefully manage scope changes to avoid breaking functionality.

Clean code principles emphasize readability and simplicity. Shadowing violates these principles by introducing unnecessary confusion and complexity. Consistent naming conventions and clear variable scopes help in writing maintainable and readable code. Shadowing disrupts this consistency.

Example of Variable Shadowing

Here's an example demonstrating how variable shadowing can cause confusion. In this example:
• The "total" variable inside the if` block shadows the "total" variable declared in the function scope.
• This shadowing can lead to confusion when trying to understand which `total` is being referenced in different parts of the function.

```
function calculateTotal(price: number, discount: number):
number {
   let total = price - discount;
   // Nested block
   if (true) {
      let total = 10; // Shadowing the outer `total` variable
      console.log('Inner total:', total); // Prints: 10
   }
   console.log('Outer total:', total); // Prints: price - discount
   return total;
}
```

Best Practices to Avoid Shadowing

Choose clear and descriptive names for variables that reflect their purpose and avoid reuse of names within different scopes.

Declare variables in the smallest scope necessary. This minimizes the risk of shadowing and helps keep the code organized.

Use naming conventions or prefixes to differentiate between variables in different scopes if shadowing is unavoidable.

Break down complex functions into smaller, more manageable functions to reduce the chance of variable shadowing.

Avoiding variable shadowing is crucial for maintaining code clarity, reducing errors, and ensuring good software practices. By using distinct, descriptive variable names and limiting their scope, you make your code more readable, maintainable, and less prone to bugs. Following this clean code rule helps ensure that your code remains understandable and easier to work with, both for you and others who may interact with it in the future.

Using Named Exports Instead of Default Exports

When developing applications with TypeScript, you have the choice between using named exports and default exports. Both have their use cases, but named exports offer several advantages, especially in large-scale projects and collaborative environments.

Named exports make it clear what is being imported from a module, improving code readability and maintainability.

```
// WrongComponent.tsx - misspelled or wrong filename
export function RightComponent(){ ... };
export default RightComponent;
// Good
import { RightComponent } from './WrongComponent';
// Bad
import WrongComponent from './WrongComponent';
```

Named exports provide better support for refactoring tools and auto-completion features in modern IDEs. For example, when renaming a named export, the IDE can automatically update all import statements across the project. This reduces the risk of errors during refactoring and speeds up the development process.

Named exports help avoid conflicts by using unique names for each export. This allows you to import and use functions with the same name from different modules without conflicts.

```
// moduleA.ts
export function fetchData() { /* ... */ };
// moduleB.ts
export function fetchData() { /* ... */ };
// usage
import { fetchData as fetchDataFromA } from './moduleA';
import { fetchData as fetchDataFromB } from './moduleB';
```

Named exports enable better tree shaking, allowing bundlers like Webpack to eliminate unused code from the final bundle.

```
// utils.ts
export const add = (a: number, b: number) => a + b;
export const subtract = (a: number, b: number) => a - b;
export const multiply = (a: number, b: number) => a * b;
// usage - only the "add" function will be included in the
final bundle, reducing the overall bundle size
import { add } from './utils';
```

Named exports lead to consistent import syntax, making the codebase more predictable and easier to understand. Developers do not need to remember the default export name, leading to fewer errors and more consistent code.

```
// constants.ts
export const PI = 3.14;
export const E = 2.71;
// usage
import { PI, E } from './constants';
```

Named exports allow you to alias imports for better readability and to avoid naming conflicts. This flexibility makes the code more readable and helps avoid conflicts with existing variables or functions.

```
// salary.ts
export function calculate() { /* ... */ };
// usage
import { calculate as calculateSalary } from './salary';
```

It's easier to add new exports to a module without breaking existing imports. Existing code remains unchanged and functional.

```
// initial version of utils.ts
export const add = (a: number, b: number) => a + b;
// later version of utils.ts
export const add = (a: number, b: number) => a + b;
export const divide = (a: number, b: number) => a / b;
// usage - it remains unchanged
import { add } from './utils';
```

Using named exports in TypeScript and React projects provides numerous advantages in terms of clarity, maintainability, IDE support, tree shaking, and overall project consistency. By promoting a more explicit and clear codebase, named exports help developers better understand, maintain, and scale their applications.

Imports

Group imports by their source, typically in the following order: external libraries, internal modules, relative imports.

```
import React from 'react';        // External libraries
import { useDispatch } from 'redux';  // Internal modules
import MyComponent from './MyComponent'; // Relative
imports
```

Prefer absolute imports over relative imports for internal modules to avoid deep relative paths and make refactoring easier. Use path aliases in your project configuration (like `tsconfig.json` or `webpack.config.js`) to create cleaner and more manageable absolute imports.

```
// Instead of this
import MyService from '../../services/MyService';
// Use this with an alias defined in tsconfig.json
import MyService from '@/services/MyService';
```

Avoid using wildcard (`* as`) imports to improve clarity and tree-shaking. Explicitly import only what is needed.

```
// Avoid this
import * as Utils from './utils';
// Prefer this
import { formatDate, parseDate } from './utils';
```

Combine imports from the same module into a single statement to reduce redundancy and clutter.

```
// Avoid this
import { useState } from 'react';
```

```
import { useEffect } from 'react';
// Prefer this
import { useState, useEffect } from 'react';
```

Remove any imports that are not used in the file to keep the codebase clean and reduce potential confusion.

```
// If formatDate is not used in the file, remove this import
import { formatDate } from 'utils/dateUtils';
```

Prefer named exports over default exports in the modules you import from, as it provides better clarity and easier refactoring.

```
// In the module file
export const calculateSum = (a: number, b: number) => a +
b;
// In the importing file
import { calculateSum } from 'utils/mathUtils';
```

Ensure all import statements are at the top of the file, separated by a blank line from the rest of the code.

```
import React, { useState } from 'react';

const MyComponent = () => {
  // Component logic here
};
```

Structure imports to avoid circular dependencies, which can lead to unexpected behavior and difficult-to-debug issues.

```
If `ModuleA` imports from `ModuleB`, ensure
`ModuleB` does not import back from `ModuleA`.
```

Do not import modules that are not explicitly listed in your project's `package.json` file. These modules may be installed as indirect dependencies by other packages, which could change or be removed during a refactor, causing your code to break unexpectedly.

```
// Avoid this if lodash is not explicitly listed in your package.json
import { debounce } from 'lodash';
// Instead, add lodash to your package.json or refactor your code.
```

Be specific with imports to avoid bringing in unnecessary code, especially when working with large libraries.

```
// Instead of importing the entire library
import _ from 'lodash';
// Import only the necessary functions
import { debounce, throttle } from 'lodash';
```

Self-Documenting Code

In software development, maintaining clear and understandable code is crucial for long-term success. Self-documenting code and useful comments are two practices that significantly contribute to this goal. Both approaches help developers understand the codebase, facilitate maintenance, and improve collaboration.

Self-documenting code refers to writing code that is easy to understand without needing extensive comments. It involves using meaningful names, clear logic, and straightforward structures.

Code that is easy to read reduces the cognitive load on developers. Developers can quickly understand what the code does, making it easier to work with.

```
// Good: Self-documenting code
function getUserFullName(user: User): string {
  return `${user.firstName} ${user.lastName}`;
};
// Bad: Unclear code
function fn(u: User): string {
  return `${u.f} ${u.l}`;
};
```

With clear code, fewer comments are needed, reducing the risk of outdated or misleading comments. Less reliance on comments makes the codebase cleaner and easier to maintain.

```
// Clear, descriptive function name
function calculateTotalPrice(items: Item[]): number {
  return items.reduce((total, item) => total + item.price, 0);
};
```

Simple and clear code is easier to debug and troubleshoot. Allows for faster identification of issues, leading to quicker resolutions.

```
// Clear variable names and logic
function isUserLoggedIn(session: Session): boolean {
  return session.isActive;
};
```

Clear code promotes better collaboration among team members. Team members can understand and contribute to the codebase more effectively.

```
// Descriptive function and variable names
function getActiveUsers(users: User[]): User[] {
  return users.filter(user => user.isActive);
};
```

Clear and well-structured code is easier to refactor and extend. Simplifies making changes and improvements to the codebase.

```
// Clear and modular code structure
function getDiscountedPrice(price: number, discount: number): number {
  return price * (1 - discount);
};
```

Writing Useful Comments

While self-documenting code reduces the need for comments, useful comments are still essential for explaining complex logic, providing context, and offering guidance.

Comments can provide background information or explain why certain decisions were made. Helps future developers understand the rationale behind specific code implementations.

```
// Fetch user data and handle edge cases for legacy
support
async function fetchUserData(userId: string):
Promise<User> {
  // API call to fetch user data
  const response = await fetch(/api/users/${userId});
  // Handle potential API changes
  if (response.status === 404) {
    throw new Error(User not found);
  }
  return response.json();
};
```

Comments can explain intricate logic that may not be immediately apparent. Makes complex sections of code more understandable, reducing the likelihood of errors.

```
// Calculate the factorial of a number using recursion
function factorial(n: number): number {
  if (n === 0) return 1;
  return n * factorial(n - 1);
```

```
};
```

Comments can document assumptions and constraints that are not evident from the code alone. Helps developers understand the context and limitations of the code, preventing misuse.

```
// Assumes user data has been validated before this
function is called
    function createUserProfile(user: User): UserProfile {
    // Function logic here
    };
```

Comments can provide guidance for future development and highlight areas for improvement. Offers direction and focus for ongoing and future development efforts.

```
// TODO: Refactor to use more efficient sorting algorithm
    function sortItems(items: Item[]): Item[] {
    return items.sort((a, b) => a.price - b.price);
    };
```

Comments can highlight critical information or potential pitfalls. Alerts developers to important details, reducing the risk of unintended consequences.

```
// WARNING: This function modifies the input array
    function sortInPlace(items: Item[]): Item[] {
    return items.sort((a, b) => a.price - b.price);
    };
```

Best Practices for Self-Documenting Code and Useful Comments

Choose names that clearly describe the purpose of variables, functions, and components.

```
const isAuthenticated =
checkUserAuthentication(session);
```

Avoid unnecessary complexity and keep the code as simple as possible.

```
const isEven = (num: number): boolean => num % 2 ===
0;
```

Focus comments on explaining why something is done, not what the code does.

```
// Using a binary search for better performance on large
arrays
```

Regularly review and update comments to ensure they remain accurate and relevant. Remove outdated comments during code refactoring.

Do not state the obvious or repeat information that is clear from the code itself.

```
// Good: No redundant comment
const userAge = 25;
// Bad: Redundant comment
const userAge = 25; // Assign 25 to userAge
```

By following these best practices, you can leverage the benefits of self-documenting code and useful comments, leading to a more maintainable, understandable, and collaborative codebase.

Consistent Formatting

Consistent formatting is crucial for maintaining a clean and manageable codebase. By adhering to a uniform coding style, developers can improve readability, reduce errors, and facilitate better collaboration. Here are the key benefits of consistent formatting:

Consistent formatting makes the code easier to read and scan through. Developers can quickly understand the structure and flow of the code.

```
// Consistently formatted code
async function fetchData(url: string): Promise<Response> {
  try {
    const response = await fetch(url);
    if (!response.ok) {
      throw new Error('Network response was not ok');
    }
    return response.json();
  } catch (error) {
    console.error('Fetch error:', error);
    throw error;
  }
};
```

Consistent formatting helps avoid common mistakes such as missing braces, misaligned code, or inconsistent indentation. Reduces the likelihood of syntax errors and logical mistakes.

```
if (isAuthenticated) {
  showUserProfile();
} else {
  redirectToLogin();
}
```

A consistent code style across the team ensures that all developers are on the same page. Facilitates smoother code reviews and easier onboarding of new team members. Use a common style guide (e.g., Airbnb, Google) and enforcing it with tools like ESLint and Prettier.

```
// .eslintrc.json
{
  "extends": ["airbnb", "plugin:@typescript-
eslint/recommended"],
  "rules": {
    "quotes": ["error", "single"],
    "semi": ["error", "always"]
  }
}
```

Uniform formatting makes it easier to maintain and update the code. Simplifies navigating the codebase and making changes. Adhere to a consistent style for function declarations, imports, and component structures.

```
// Consistent function and component structure
export function Button({ onClick, children }) (
  <button onClick={onClick}>{children}</button>
);
```

Tools like Prettier can automatically format code according to the specified style, reducing manual formatting efforts.

Saves time and ensures consistent formatting across the codebase.

```
# Install Prettier
npm install --save-dev prettier
# .prettierrc
{
  "singleQuote": true,
  "semi": true,
  "trailingComma": "all"
}
# Format code
npx prettier --write src/
```

Consistent formatting leads to cleaner diffs in version control systems like Git, making it easier to review changes. Simplifies code reviews and reduces noise in diffs.

```
# Git diff with consistent formatting
git diff
```

Professionalism and Code Quality

Consistently formatted code reflects a high standard of professionalism and attention to detail. Demonstrates commitment to quality and best practices, which can positively impact team morale and codebase reputation.

```
// Well-formatted code
function calculateTotalPrice(items: Item[]): number {
  return items.reduce((total, item) => total + item.price, 0);
};
```

Best Practices for Consistent Formatting

Choose a well-known style guide (e.g., Airbnb, Google) and

stick to it.

Configure ESLint for linting and Prettier for formatting.

```
// .eslintrc.json
{
  "extends": ["plugin:react/recommended",
"plugin:@typescript-eslint/recommended"],
  "rules": {
    "react/jsx-filename-extension": [1, { "extensions": [".tsx"] }],
    "semi": ["error", "always"]
  }
}
// .prettierrc
{
  "singleQuote": true,
  "trailingComma": "all"
}
```

Use blank lines to visually separate distinct sections or concepts within your code. This practice helps make the code more readable by clearly distinguishing between different blocks of logic, functions, or responsibilities. For example, separating variable declarations, function definitions, or logical sections of a function with blank lines makes it easier for others to quickly understand the flow and structure of the code.

Code that is logically related should be grouped closely together, with minimal vertical space between them. This "vertical density" ensures that related concepts are easily identifiable as part of the same functionality or process. By keeping related code together, you reduce the cognitive load on readers and help prevent misunderstandings about how different parts of the code interact.

Horizontal openness refers to the practice of adding spaces around operators (such as =, +, -, *) and after commas in lists or function arguments. This improves readability by preventing code from looking cramped and by making the individual components of expressions more distinguishable. Proper horizontal spacing allows developers to quickly parse and understand expressions, leading to fewer errors and more maintainable code.

Consistent indentation is essential for visually representing the structure and hierarchy of your code. Proper indentation makes it clear where blocks of code begin and end, how different sections of code relate to each other, and which statements are nested within others. This clarity is crucial for understanding control flow, especially in complex functions or nested loops. Consistent indentation across the codebase also promotes uniformity, making it easier for teams to collaborate and maintain the code.

Use pre-commit hooks to enforce formatting before code is committed.

```
# Install husky and lint-staged
npm install --save-dev husky lint-staged
# package.json
{
  "husky": {
```

```
  "hooks": {
    "pre-commit": "lint-staged"
  }
},
  "lint-staged": {
    "src/**/*.{js,jsx,ts,tsx}": ["eslint --fix", "prettier --write"]
  }
}
```

Regularly review the formatting guidelines and update them as necessary to incorporate best practices.

By adhering to these practices, you can ensure that your TypeScript codebase remains clean, readable, and maintainable, leading to more efficient development processes and higher quality software.

Explicit Types

TypeScript enhances JavaScript by adding a type system that can greatly improve code quality and maintainability. Both explicit types and type inference are crucial features in TypeScript, and each offers distinct benefits. Understanding how to leverage these features effectively can lead to more robust and reliable code in your applications. Explicit types involve explicitly specifying the types of variables, function parameters, and return values. This approach provides clear and predictable type information.

Explicitly defining types makes the code more readable and helps other developers understand the expected types at a glance. Reduces ambiguity and clarifies what type of data is expected and returned.

```
// Explicit type declaration
function greetUser(userName: string): string {
  return `Hello, ${userName}!`;
};
```

Explicit types help catch type-related errors at compile time rather than runtime, improving overall type safety. Minimizes runtime errors related to incorrect data types.

```
// Function with explicit types
function addNumbers(a: number, b: number): number {
  return a + b;
};
```

```
// Error if passing a string
addNumbers(5, '10'); // Error: Argument of type 'string' is
not assignable to parameter of type 'number'.
```

Explicit types act as documentation for functions and components, making it easier for others to understand how they should be used. Provides a clear contract for what data the component expects, improving maintainability.

```
// Explicit type for a React component's props
interface UserProfileProps {
  userId: string;
  age: number;
}
function UserProfile({ userId, age }: UserProfileProps) {
  // Component implementation
};
```

Explicit types improve IDE support, such as autocompletion and inline documentation. IDEs can offer better autocompletion and type checking, enhancing the development experience.

```
function fetchData(url: string): Promise<Response> {
  return fetch(url);
};
```

Explicit types help maintain consistent APIs, making it easier to integrate with other parts of the system or third-party libraries. Ensures that the function returns the expected type, which is crucial for integration and debugging.

```
// Explicit return type for API functions
function fetchUserById(id: string): Promise<User> {
  // API call to fetch user
};
```

Law of Demeter: types should avoid "talking" to too many other types, keeping interactions minimal and to direct collaborators.

Type Inference

Type inference is TypeScript's ability to automatically determine the type of a variable or expression when it's not explicitly provided. While explicit types are helpful, type inference offers its own set of advantages.

Type inference reduces the need for redundant type annotations, making the code less verbose and more concise. Simplifies the code, especially in cases where the type is obvious from the context.

```
// TypeScript infers the type
const message = 'Hello, world!'; // Type inferred as string
```

Type inference allows for more flexible and less rigid code while still providing type safety. Enables you to write more adaptable code without losing type safety.

```
const numbers = [1, 2, 3]; // Type inferred as number[]
```

TypeScript automatically updates inferred types when code changes, reducing the need for manual type adjustments. Ensures that type information stays accurate as the code evolves.

```
const getUser = () => ({ name: 'Alice', age: 30 }); // Type inferred as { name: string; age: number }
```

Type inference reduces the cognitive load on developers by automatically determining types where the context is

59

clear. Developers can focus on logic rather than managing type annotations.

```
const add = (a: number, b: number) => a + b; // Return type
inferred as number
```

TypeScript can infer complex types, such as union types or function signatures, making it easier to work with advanced TypeScript features. Facilitates working with complex data structures without explicit type annotations.

```
function processResult(result: string | number) {
  if (typeof result === 'string') {
    // Handle string
  } else {
    // Handle number
  }
};
```

Best Practices for Using Explicit Types and Type Inference

For public APIs, function signatures, and complex logic, use explicit types to ensure clarity and safety.

For simple variables and straightforward expressions, let TypeScript infer the types to keep the code concise.

Find a balance that leverages the strengths of both explicit typing and type inference to maintain code readability and safety.

Adjust TypeScript compiler options to control how strict the type inference is, such as enabling `strict` mode for better type safety.

By effectively utilizing explicit types and type inference, you can harness the full power of TypeScript to write clear, maintainable, and reliable code in your React applications.

Small Files Size

As a clean code rule, aim to keep your files small and focused, ideally under 200–300 lines. A smaller file size helps maintain readability, makes it easier to navigate the codebase, and encourages better organization by naturally grouping related functions, components, or classes together.

Smaller files are easier to read and understand, allowing developers to quickly grasp the purpose and functionality.

It encourages adhering to the Single Responsibility Principle (SRP), where each file handles one aspect or feature of the application.

It becomes easier to locate and manage code, reducing the time spent searching through large files.

Smaller files reduce merge conflicts in version control systems, making it easier for multiple developers to work on the codebase simultaneously.

Keeping files small and focused helps maintain a clean, manageable, and scalable codebase. But there can be too many so it's important to group them in a way that maintains order and improves navigation. Here are some strategies:

Organize files into directories based on features or modules (e.g., "user", "auth", "dashboard"). This keeps related files together, making it easier to find all code relevant to a particular feature.

```
/src
 /user
  User.tsx
  User.types.ts
  User.style.ts
  User.consts.ts
  User.utils.ts
 /auth
  Auth.tsx
  Auth.types.ts
  Auth.style.ts
```

Organize files by their role in the application architecture, such as "components", "services", "utils", "hooks", etc. This helps keep the structure logical and clear, especially in larger applications.

```
/src
 /components
  /user
   User.tsx
   User.types.ts
 /services
  api.service.ts
  auth.service.ts
 /hooks
  useAuth.ts
  useUser.ts
```

For larger, more complex applications, consider organizing by business domain (e.g., "orders", "customers", "products"). Each domain contains its own subdirectories for components, services, types, etc.

```
/src
 /orders
  components
  services
  types
 /customers
  components
  services
  types
```

For reusable components, utilities, or constants that are used across multiple features, have a "shared" or "common" directory.

```
/src
 /shared
  components
   Button.tsx
   Modal.tsx
  utils
   formatDate.ts
   parseUrl.ts
```

In directories with many small files, use "index.ts" files to re-export items, simplifying imports and reducing clutter in other parts of the application.

```
/src
 /components
  /user
   index.ts // Re-exports User, etc.
   User.tsx
```

User.types.ts

Use consistent and descriptive naming conventions for files and directories. This helps developers understand the purpose of files and their relationships at a glance.

Within a feature or domain directory, create subdirectories like "components", "services", "types", and "styles" to further organize related files.

```
/src
 /user
  /components
    UserList.tsx
    UserProfile.tsx
  /services
    userService.ts
  /types
    user.types.ts
```

By grouping files effectively based on these strategies, you can maintain a clean, organized codebase that scales well even with a large number of small files.

Single Responsibility Principle (SRP)

The Single Responsibility Principle states that a module, class, or function should have only one reason to change, meaning it should have only one job or responsibility. In the context of TypeScript and React, this principle applies to functions, components, and even modules.

Each function or component has a clear purpose, making the code easier to read and understand. Developers can quickly grasp what each part of the code does without having to dig through complex logic.

```
// Good: Separate responsibilities
function fetchUserData(userId: string) {
  // Fetch user data from API
}
function renderUserProfile(userData: User) {
  // Render user profile UI
}
```

Functions and components with single responsibilities are more reusable across different parts of the application. Promotes code reuse, reducing duplication and improving consistency.

```
// Reusable data fetching function
function fetchData(endpoint: string) {
  return fetch(endpoint).then(response => response.json());
}
// Reusable UI component
function UserProfile({ user }: { user: User }) (
```

```
<div>{user.name}</div>
);
```

Functions and components with single responsibilities are easier to test in isolation. Simplifies writing and maintaining tests, leading to better test coverage and more robust code.

```
// Test fetchUserData function separately
test('fetchUserData fetches user data', () => {
  // Arrange, Act, Assert
});
// Test UserProfile component separately
test('UserProfile renders user name', () => {
  // Arrange, Act, Assert
});
```

When a function or component has a single responsibility, changes are more localized and less likely to introduce bugs. Facilitates safer and more efficient debugging and refactoring.

```
// Good: Change only data fetching logic
function fetchUserData(userId: string) {
  // Updated fetch logic
}
```

Small Functions and Components

Small functions and components align well with Single Responsibility Principle, emphasizing the need to break down complex logic into manageable, understandable pieces.

Small functions and components are easier to read and understand. Reduces cognitive load on developers, making the codebase more approachable.

```
// Good: Small, focused function
function calculateDiscount(price: number, discount:
number): number {
  return price * (1 - discount);
}
```

Small, focused functions and components are more reusable across different parts of the application. Encourages the use of modular, reusable code, leading to a more DRY (Don't Repeat Yourself) codebase.

```
// Reusable button component
function Button({ onClick, children }: PropsWithChildren<{
onClick: () => void }>) (
  <button onClick={onClick}>{children}</button>
);
```

Small functions and components are easier to test individually. Improves test coverage and ensures more reliable code.

```
// Test small, focused function
test('calculateDiscount calculates correct discount', () => {
  expect(calculateDiscount(100, 0.1)).toBe(90);
});
```

Small functions and components limit the scope of bugs, making them easier to locate and fix. Simplifies debugging and reduces the risk of introducing new bugs during maintenance.

```
// Good: Small component with clear responsibility
function UserProfile({ user }: { user: User }) (
  <div>{user.name}</div>
);
```

Small, focused React components can help optimize rendering performance by reducing unnecessary re-renders. Enhances application performance, especially in large, complex UIs.

```
const MemoizedButton = React.memo(Button);
```

Small components with focused responsibilities make it easier to manage and understand props and state. Simplifies the management of data flow and state, leading to fewer bugs and better encapsulation.

```
// Good: Separate components for input and display
function UserInput({ onInput }: { onInput: (input: string) =>
void }) (
  <input onChange={(e) => onInput(e.target.value)} />
);
function UserDisplay({ user }: { user: User }) (
  <div>{user.name}</div>
);
```

Applying the Single Responsibility Principle and keeping functions and components small provides numerous benefits. These practices lead to more readable, maintainable, reusable, and testable code, ultimately resulting in higher quality and more scalable applications. By breaking down complex logic into manageable pieces and ensuring that each piece has a clear, focused responsibility, developers can create robust and efficient codebases that are easier to work with and evolve over time.

Separation of Concerns

Separation of Concerns refers to the practice of organizing code so that distinct sections handle different aspects of the functionality. This principle helps in dividing the application into distinct features or modules, each managing its own responsibilities.

By separating concerns, changes to one part of the application have minimal impact on others. Simplifies updating or fixing bugs in specific areas without affecting unrelated parts.

```
// Separate data fetching logic from UI components
async function fetchUserData(userId: string):
Promise<User> {
    const response = await fetch(`/api/users/${userId}`);
    return response.json();
};
function UserProfile({ userId }: { userId: string }) {
    const [user, setUser] = useState<User | null>(null);
    useEffect(() => {
        fetchUserData(userId).then(setUser);
    }, [userId]);
    if (!user) return <div>Loading...</div>;
    return <div>{user.name}</div>;
};
```

Clear separation of different functionalities makes the codebase easier to read and understand. Enhances comprehension and ease of navigation within the code.

```
// Separate concerns in a React component
function LoginForm() {
  const [username, setUsername] = React.useState('');
  const [password, setPassword] = React.useState('');
  const handleSubmit = (event: React.FormEvent) => {
    event.preventDefault();
    // Handle form submission
  };
  return (
    <form onSubmit={handleSubmit}>
      <input
        type="text"
        value={username}
        onChange={(e) => setUsername(e.target.value)}
      />
      <input
        type="password"
        value={password}
        onChange={(e) => setPassword(e.target.value)}
      />
      <button type="submit">Login</button>
    </form>
  );
};
```

Each module or component can be tested independently, improving the focus and effectiveness of tests. Simplifies testing and ensures each part of the code functions correctly.

```
// Testing the fetchUserData function
test('fetchUserData returns user data', async () => {
  const userId = '123';
  const mockUser = { name: 'John Doe' };
  global.fetch = jest.fn(() =>
    Promise.resolve({ json: () => Promise.resolve(mockUser)
})
```

```
) as jest.Mock;
const user = await fetchUserData(userId);
expect(user.name).toBe('John Doe');
});
```

Different team members can work on separate concerns simultaneously without interfering with each other's work. Enhances productivity and reduces merge conflicts

```
// Separate components and services
// Service: userService.ts
async function getUser(id: string) { /*...*/ };
// Component: UserProfile.tsx
function UserProfile() { /*...*/ };
```

As the application grows, well-separated concerns facilitate easier scalability and extension. Simplifies integrating new features or components without disrupting existing functionality.

```
// Adding a new feature, e.g., user notifications
function UserNotifications() {
  // Fetch and display user notifications
};
```

Reusability

Reusability refers to the practice of designing components or functions so that they can be used in multiple contexts without modification. This principle reduces redundancy and promotes efficiency.

Reusable components and functions help avoid duplicating code, leading to a more efficient codebase. Minimizes redundancy and simplifies code maintenance.

```
// Reusable button component
function Button({ onClick, children }:
PropsWithChildren<{ onClick: () => void }>) (
    <button onClick={onClick}>{children}</button>
);
// Usage in different parts of the app
const SubmitButton: React.FC = () => <Button
onClick={handleSubmit}>Submit</Button>;
    const CancelButton: React.FC = () => <Button
onClick={handleCancel}>Cancel</Button>;
```

Reusable UI components ensure consistency across different parts of the application. Provides a consistent user interface and experience throughout the application.

```
// Reusable input field component
function TextInput({ value, onChange }: { value: string;
onChange: (e: React.ChangeEvent<HTMLInputElement>) =>
void }) (
    <input type="text" value={value} onChange={onChange}
/>
);
```

Reusing existing components or functions accelerates development and reduces the need for creating new code from scratch. Speeds up development by leveraging pre-built components.

```
// Reusing a modal component
function Modal({ isOpen, onClose }: { isOpen: boolean;
onClose: () => void }) (
    isOpen ? (
      <div className="modal">
       <button onClick={onClose}>Close</button>
      </div>
    ) : null
);
```

Updating a reusable component or function in one place automatically reflects changes throughout the application. Simplifies maintenance and ensures consistency with fewer changes.

```
// Updating reusable component styles
function Button({ onClick, children }:
PropsWithChildren<{ onClick: () => void }>) (
    <button className="btn-primary"
onClick={onClick}>{children}</button>
);
```

Testing reusable components or functions in isolation ensures they work correctly in various scenarios. Ensures that reusable components are reliable and behave as expected.

```
// Testing reusable button component
test('Button click triggers onClick handler', () => {
```

```
const handleClick = jest.fn();
render(<Button onClick={handleClick}>Click
Me</Button>);
fireEvent.click(screen.getByText('Click Me'));
expect(handleClick).toHaveBeenCalledTimes(1);
});
```

Best Practices for Separation of Concerns and Reusability

Ensure each component or module handles one specific aspect of the application's functionality.

Design components to be generic and reusable across different parts of the application.

Use services or custom hooks to encapsulate business logic and data-fetching logic separate from UI components.

Organize the codebase into modules or features, each managing its own concern, to improve maintainability.

Provide clear documentation for reusable components and functions to facilitate their usage and understanding.

By adhering to the principles of Separation of Concerns and Reusability, you can build more organized, maintainable, and scalable React applications.

Number of Arguments

One of the key principles of clean code is to minimize the number of arguments in functions. Here's an explanation of why this is important and how to apply it effectively, especially in the context of TypeScript and React development.

Functions with fewer arguments are easier to read and understand. They clearly express their purpose without overwhelming the reader with too many details.

Functions with fewer parameters are easier to use correctly. When a function requires many arguments, it increases the likelihood of errors and misuse.

Code with simpler functions is easier to maintain and refactor. It is straightforward to understand what each function does and how it interacts with the rest of the code.

Functions with fewer arguments are easier to test. Fewer arguments mean fewer combinations of inputs to consider when writing tests.

Recommended Practices

Ideally, functions should have zero, one, or two arguments.

Three can be acceptable but should be avoided if possible. Functions with more than three arguments are typically considered problematic.

When a function requires multiple related arguments, consider encapsulating them in an object. This not only reduces the number of parameters but also makes the code more expressive.

```
// Without object grouping
function createUser(name: string, age: number, email:
string) {...}
// With object grouping
type UserInfo = {
  name: string;
  age: number;
  email: string;
}
function createUser(user: UserInfo) { ... }
```

In TypeScript and React, destructuring can make the function signatures more readable and the code inside the function cleaner.

```
type UserInfo = {
  name: string;
  age: number;
  email: string;
}
function createUser({ name, age, email }: UserInfo) { ... }
```

TypeScript allows for optional parameters and default values, which can simplify function signatures.

```
function greet(name: string, greeting: string = "Hello") {
  console.log(`${greeting}, ${name}!`);
}
greet("Alice"); // Output: Hello, Alice!
```

Avoid passing null to functions. Use optional parameters or default values instead.

If a function seems to require many arguments, it might be doing too much. Consider breaking it down into smaller, more focused functions.

```
// Function doing too much
function processUserData(name: string, age: number,
email: string, address: string, isActive: boolean) { ... }
// Broken down into smaller functions
function validateUser(name: string, age: number, email:
string) {
  // validation logic
}
function saveUser(name: string, email: string) {
  // save logic
}
function notifyUser(email: string, isActive: boolean) {
  // notification logic
}
// Then use these smaller functions as needed
```

Application in React Components

In React, this principle can also be applied to component props. Components with fewer props are easier to use and understand.

For complex components, pass a single object containing related props.

```
// Without object grouping
function UserCard({ name, age, email }) {
  return (
   <div>
    <h2>{name}</h2>
    <p>Age: {age}</p>
    <p>Email: {email}</p>
   </div>
  );
}
// With object grouping
function UserCard({ user }) {
  return (
   <div>
    <h2>{user.name}</h2>
    <p>Age: {user.age}</p>
    <p>Email: {user.email}</p>
   </div>
  );
}
```

For data that needs to be accessed by many components, consider using React Context or Redux Toolkit to avoid prop drilling.

Minimizing the number of arguments in functions is a crucial practice that enhances readability, maintainability, and testability. By aiming to keep functions simple and focused, encapsulating related arguments in objects, and leveraging features like destructuring and default values, developers can write cleaner and more efficient code.

Defining Return Types for Utility Functions

In TypeScript, explicitly defining the return type of functions, especially utility functions, is considered a best practice. This practice enhances code quality, readability, maintainability, and robustness. Here's why it's good to define the return type for utility functions in TypeScript:

Specifying the return type makes it clear to anyone reading the code what the function is expected to return. This improves readability and helps other developers (and your future self) understand the function's behavior without having to delve into its implementation. Explicit return types serve as inline documentation, reducing the need for additional comments and making the code self-explanatory.

```
// Clear and understandable
function getUserName(userId: string): string {
  // Implementation
}
```

When the return type is explicitly defined, it ensures that the function consistently returns the expected type, even if the implementation changes. This consistency aids in maintaining the code over time. During refactoring, explicit return types act as a safeguard, ensuring that any changes to the function's logic do not inadvertently alter the expected return type. This reduces the risk of introducing bugs.

TypeScript's type-checking capabilities can only be fully utilized when return types are explicitly defined. The TypeScript compiler can then verify that the function returns the correct type, catching potential errors at compile time rather than at runtime. Explicit return types help prevent common mistakes, such as returning "null" or "undefined" when a value of a different type is expected. This makes the code more robust and less prone to bugs.

```
// TypeScript will raise an error if the return type does not match
function calculateTotal(price: number, tax: number): number {
  return price + tax;
}
```

Modern IDEs like Visual Studio Code provide better IntelliSense support (autocomplete, type hints, etc.) when return types are explicitly defined. This improves the developer experience by providing accurate type information and suggestions. IDEs can better navigate the code, provide accurate jump-to-definition features, and generate more useful inline documentation when return types are specified.

When functions are composed together, knowing their return types explicitly helps in chaining functions and ensures that the output of one function can be seamlessly used as the input for another. For utility functions used across different parts of an application or even different applications, defining return types establishes a clear contract. This contract ensures that the consuming code knows exactly what to expect.

```
// Chaining functions with known return types
function parseJson(jsonString: string): object {
  return JSON.parse(jsonString);
}
function getUserData(): string {
  // Fetch user data as JSON string
}
const userData: object = parseJson(getUserData());
```

Clean code principles advocate for explicitness and clarity. Defining return types aligns with these principles by making the code's intent and behavior explicit. Clear return types minimize surprises for anyone using the function, as they set explicit expectations about what the function returns.

Example

Without Explicit Return Type

```
function fetchData(url: string) {
  // Implementation
  return fetch(url).then(response => response.json());
}
// Usage
const data = fetchData("https://api.example.com/data"); //
Type is inferred
```

With Explicit Return Type

```
function fetchData(url: string): Promise<any> {
  // Implementation
  return fetch(url).then(response => response.json());
}
// Usage
const data: Promise<any> =
fetchData("https://api.example.com/data"); // Type is explicit
```

In the second example, the explicit return type "Promise<any>" makes it clear that "fetchData" returns a promise, which helps understand how to handle the returned value properly.

Defining return types for utility functions in TypeScript is a good practice that enhances code readability, maintainability, type safety, and developer experience. It ensures consistency, aids in error detection, and aligns with clean code principles, making the codebase more robust and easier to work with.

Avoiding "if-else" Statements

Avoiding "if-else" statements is a clean code practice that promotes simpler, more readable, and maintainable code. Here is why:

"If-else" statements often lead to deep nesting, which can make the code harder to follow. By avoiding "if-else", you keep your functions flat and reduce cognitive load.

Instead of using "if-else", handling special conditions with early "return" statements (guard clauses) simplifies the flow. This makes it easier for someone reading the code to understand the main logic without getting bogged down by multiple conditions. Code becomes more expressive and intention-revealing when not cluttered with multiple branches of logic.

Rather than using "if-else" to handle different types or behaviors, you can leverage polymorphism, where different classes implement the same method in their own way. This leads to more modular and testable code. You can replace complex conditional logic with design patterns like the Strategy Pattern, where you select an algorithm at runtime based on the situation.

Fewer conditional branches mean each function is easier to test, as you are dealing with simpler, more focused logic.

The fewer paths through your code, the less chance there is of missing a case or introducing bugs.

In summary, avoiding "if-else" statements leads to cleaner, more maintainable code by reducing complexity, enhancing readability, and encouraging better design practices.

Return as soon as possible from a function

Returning as soon as possible from a function is a clean code practice that enhances readability and maintainability. By exiting a function early when certain conditions are met, you avoid unnecessary nesting and reduce cognitive load. This makes the function easier to understand, as readers can quickly grasp the core logic without wading through layers of conditional statements. Early returns also help prevent subtle bugs by clearly defining the exit points, making the function's behavior more predictable.

Using an "if" statement followed by an immediate "return" is a clean code practice that simplifies function logic by clearly handling edge cases or exceptions upfront. This technique, known as "guard clauses," allows you to address special conditions early in the function, making the main logic more straightforward and easier to follow.

Example

```
function process(data?: Data) {
  if (!data) return;
  // Main logic continues here...
}
```

In this example, if "data" is undefined, the function exits immediately. This avoids the need for additional nesting and keeps the core logic unencumbered by special cases, improving overall code clarity and reducing the chance of errors.

An other example

```
// Bad
function processOrder(order: Order): string {
  if (order) {
    if (order.isPaid) {
     if (order.isShipped) {
      if (order.isDelivered) {
       return "Order is complete";
      } else {
       return "Order is shipped but not delivered";
      }
     } else {
      return "Order is paid but not shipped";
     }
    } else {
     return "Order is not paid";
    }
  } else {
   return "Order not found";
  }
}

// Good
function processOrder(order: Order): string {
  if (!order) {
   return "Order not found";
  }
  if (!order.isPaid) {
   return "Order is not paid";
  }
  if (!order.isShipped) {
```

```
  return "Order is paid but not shipped";
}
if (!order.isDelivered) {
  return "Order is shipped but not delivered";
}
return "Order is complete";
}
```

Organizing Functions

Functions should be organized in the order in which they are used and grouped by their purpose to enhance readability, maintainability, and logical flow.

Place the most important functions or those that are called directly from outside or at the top of the file. These are typically functions that define the main operations or behaviors of the component or module.
Place helper or utility functions that are called internally or are less critical further down in the file. This helps keep the main logic visible and easily accessible at the top.

Group functions that serve similar purposes together. For instance, group all data fetching functions together, or all event handlers together. This makes it easier to locate and understand related functions. Create logical sections in your file or module with comments or separators to delineate different types of functions, such as setup functions, core logic functions, and utility functions.

Benefits

Organizing functions in the order they are used creates a logical flow that mirrors how the component or module operates. This makes it easier for developers to follow and understand the code. Functions that are most relevant or commonly used are located at the top, making them quicker to access and understand.

When functions are grouped by purpose, it becomes simpler to update or refactor related functionality without having to sift through unrelated code. Developers can more easily grasp the structure and purpose of the codebase, reducing the cognitive load when navigating or modifying the code.

Following a consistent structure for function organization helps enforce a predictable pattern, making the codebase more intuitive and less error-prone. Grouping and ordering functions help maintain a clear separation between different concerns or functionalities within the code.

Organizing functions by the order of their use and grouping them by purpose adheres to the clean code principle of readability and maintainability. This approach ensures that the code is logically structured, making it easier to understand and work with. By placing important functions at the top and grouping related functions together, you enhance the clarity and efficiency of your codebase. You should see the code of detail functions only if you are interested.

In TypeScript, organizing variables in the order of their use is not always possible because of **hoisting** and **type dependencies**. Variables often need to be declared before they're referenced in the code, especially when they are types, interfaces, or constants that other parts of the code depend on. Additionally, TypeScript enforces strict order when it comes to using variables, requiring that declarations appear before their usage to prevent errors during compilation.

Presentational Components

In React, the Presentational and Container Components pattern is a design approach that separates concerns in a React application, leading to clearer, more maintainable code. This pattern leverages **props** for data and behavior management and **state management** for internal component logic. Understanding the benefits of this separation can enhance the quality of your React applications.

Presentational Components (also known as Dumb Components) are responsible for rendering the UI and receiving data and callbacks via props. They are often stateless and focus solely on how things look.

Presentational components are designed to be reusable in different parts of the application. For example, The Button component can be reused across different parts of the app with different labels and click handlers.

```
// Presentational component
type ButtonProps = {
  label: string;
  onClick: () => void;
}
function Button({ label, onClick }: ButtonProps) (
  <button onClick={onClick}>{label}</button>
);
```

Testing presentational components is straightforward since they are mainly concerned with rendering based on props. Easier to test since you can focus on rendering logic and UI aspects.

```
// Testing presentational component
test('Button displays the correct label', () => {
  const { getByText } = render(<Button label="Click Me"
onClick={() => {}} />);
  expect(getByText('Click Me')).toBeInTheDocument();
});
```

Presentational components handle only the visual aspects and receive data and behavior from their parent components. Ensures that the component's logic is decoupled from its appearance.

```
// Presentational component for displaying user
information
type UserCardProps = {
  name: string;
  age: number;
}
function UserCard({ name, age }: UserCardProps) (
  <div>
    <h2>{name}</h2>
    <p>Age: {age}</p>
  </div>
);
```

By using reusable presentational components, you ensure a consistent look and feel throughout the application. Promotes consistency and reduces duplication.

```
// Reusing a presentational component for different parts
```

of the application
```
    <UserCard name="Alice" age={30} />
    <UserCard name="Bob" age={25} />
```

Container Components

Container Components (also known as Smart Components) manage the state and handle logic. They interact with APIs, manage state, and pass data and callbacks down to presentational components via **props**.

Container components are responsible for managing state and logic, which can be shared with multiple presentational components. Keeps state management separate from the presentation logic, making it easier to maintain and test.

```
// Container component managing user data
function UserContainer() {
  const [user, setUser] = React.useState<User | null>(null);
  React.useEffect(() => {
   fetchUserData().then(setUser);
  }, []);
  return user ? <UserCard name={user.name}
age={user.age} /> : <div>Loading...</div>;
 };
```

Container components can be tested for their state management and logic, while presentational components focus on rendering. Facilitates testing of the state management and data flow separately from UI rendering.

```
// Testing container component logic
test('UserContainer fetches and displays user data', async
() => {
  // Mocking fetchUserData and rendering component
```

```
  // Assert that UserCard is displayed with user data
  });
```

Container components handle business logic and data-fetching, while presentational components handle UI rendering. Helps in organizing code by separating logic from presentation, improving maintainability.

```
  // Container component with business logic
  function UserContainer() {
   // State and logic here
   return <UserCard name="Alice" age={30} />;
  };
```

With a clear distinction between logic and presentation, the codebase becomes easier to scale and maintain. Simplifies making updates and scaling features without disrupting existing code.

```
  // Adding new features or updating logic
  // Only modify the container component while keeping
the presentational component unchanged
```

Container components can be reused across different parts of the application to manage similar logic and state. Promotes reusability of business logic and state management patterns.

```
  // Container for managing different types of data
  function DataContainer({ fetchData }: { fetchData: () =>
Promise<any> }) {
   const [data, setData] = React.useState<any>(null);
   React.useEffect(() => {
    fetchData().then(setData);
   }, [fetchData]);
```

```
    return data ? <DataDisplay data={data} /> :
<div>Loading...</div>;
    };
```

Best Practices for Using Presentational and Container Components

Ensure presentational components are stateless and only render based on props.

Use container components to handle data-fetching, state management, and business logic.

Use props to pass data and callbacks from container components to presentational components.

Use context to avoid props drilling.

Use shared state management (like redux) to distribute the information to different components or to produce side effects in the state for some dispatched actions.

Manage state within containers or lift state up to parent components when needed for sharing across multiple children.

Clearly define the roles of presentational and container components to keep the codebase organized and maintainable.

By effectively using the Presentational and Container Components pattern along with props and state management, you can create React applications that are easier to maintain, test, and scale, leading to a more robust and user-friendly application.

Splitting a Smart Component into Specialized Components

Splitting a React component into specialized parts - such as a routing component, data-fetching component, data-preparation component, layout component, and a dumb (or presentational) component - brings several key benefits. This approach leverages the principle of separation of concerns, making your codebase more modular, maintainable, and testable.

Routing Component

This component is responsible for extracting data from the URL and determining which part of the application to display based on route parameters.

• Separation of Concerns: Keeps routing logic separate from other concerns, simplifying the routing logic and making it easier to manage.

• Flexibility: Allows you to handle different routes and URL parameters in a centralized location, making the routing logic reusable and easier to maintain.

```
// Routing Component
function UserProfileRoute() {
  const { userId } = useParams<{ userId: string }>();
  return <UserProfileContainer userId={userId} />;
};
```

Data-Fetching Component

This component handles the actual data retrieval based on parameters extracted by the routing component.

● Encapsulation: Encapsulates data-fetching logic, making it easier to manage and test.

● Separation: Keeps data-fetching logic separate from UI rendering and state management, reducing complexity.

```
// Data-Fetching Component
function UserProfileContainer({ userId }: { userId: string }) {
  const [user, setUser] = useState<User | null>(null);
  const [loading, setLoading] = useState<boolean>(true);
  useEffect(() => {
    fetchUserData(userId).then((data) => {
      setUser(data);
      setLoading(false);
    });
  }, [userId]);
  if( !loading ){
    return <UserProfileView user={user} />;
  }
};
```

Data-Preparation Component

This component prepares or transforms the data before passing it to the presentation layer. It may handle sorting, filtering, or formatting the data.

● Data Transformation: Keeps data preparation logic separate from both data fetching and presentation, allowing for more focused and maintainable code.

● Reusability: Can be reused across different components that need similar data preparation.

```
// Data Preparation Component
function UserProfileView({ user }: { user: User }) {
 // Prepare or transform data
 const formattedUser = {
   ...user,
   formattedName: user.name.toUpperCase(),
 };
 return (
  <UserProfileLayout
  beforeUser={ <UserProfileDisplay user={user}/> }
  afterUser={ <UserProfileDisplay user={formattedUser} /> }
  />
 );
};
```

A Data-Preparation Component should have its business logic extracted into a separate file to maintain clean separation of concerns. This keeps the component focused on preparing data for presentation, while the logic itself is isolated, making it easier to test, maintain, and reuse across different parts of the application. This approach also enhances readability by keeping the component code concise and modular.

Layout Component

This component is responsible for the layout and structure of the UI, arranging child components and applying styles.
• Separation of Layout: Keeps layout logic separate from data handling and presentation, making it easier to manage and update the UI layout independently.
• Consistency: Ensures consistent application of layout and styling across different parts of the application.

```
// Layout Component
function CompareUserProfileLayout({ beforeUser,
afterUser }: { beforeUser: ReactNode, afterUser: ReactNode }){
  return (
   <div className="user-profile-layout">
    <div id="before-user">{beforeUser}</div>
    <div id="after-user">{afterUser}</div>
   </div>
  );
};
```

Dumb (or Presentational) Component

This component is solely responsible for rendering the UI based on the data provided. It receives props and renders the user interface but does not handle logic beyond rendering.

• Simplified UI: Focuses only on how data is presented, making it easy to understand and maintain.

• Reusability: Can be reused across different parts of the application with different data.

• Testability: Easier to test as it only concerns itself with rendering and does not include complex logic. You can use snapshot testing to verify their rendering. Snapshot tests capture the output of a component at a given time and compare it against future renderings to ensure consistency. This is particularly effective, as the main responsibility of dumb components is rendering UI based on props, making them ideal candidates for snapshot testing to quickly catch unintended changes in the UI.

```
// Dumb Component
   function UserProfileDisplay({ user }: { user: User & {
formattedName?: string } }) (
     <div>
       <h1>{user.formattedName || user.name}</h1>
       <p>{user.email}</p>
     </div>
   );
```

How These Components Work Together

● Routing Component
Extracts the URL parameters and passes them to the data-fetching component.

● Data-Fetching Component
Uses the parameters to fetch data and then provides it to the data-preparation component.

● Data-Preparation Component
Prepares the data and sends it to the layout component.

● Layout Component
Manages the overall structure and layout of the UI, including rendering the dumb component with the prepared data.

● Dumb Component
Receives the data and renders the UI.

Benefices

Smaller components with single responsibilities make it easier to refactor code. Changes in one component have a minimal impact on others. Facilitates safer and more controlled changes to the codebase.

```
// Refactoring the data fetching logic
const useUserData = (userId: string) => {
  // Code for fetching data
};
```

Breaking down components allows for more granular control over rendering. For instance, React's memo can be used to prevent unnecessary re-renders of components. Or you can use suspense for a better user experience. Improves performance by avoiding unnecessary renders and optimizing component updates.

```
// Memoized UserProfileDisplay component
const UserProfileDisplay: FC<{ user: User }> = memo(({ user
}) => (
  <div>
    <h1>{user.name}</h1>
    <p>{user.email}</p>
  </div>
));
```

Each component handles a specific aspect of the application, such as routing, data fetching, or rendering. This separation makes it easier to manage and understand each part of the component. Ensures that each component has a clear and focused role, which enhances the maintainability and readability of the code.

```
// Routing component
function UserProfileRoute() {
  const { userId } = useParams<{ userId: string }>();
  return <UserProfileContainer userId={userId} />;
};
// Data fetching component
function UserProfileContainer({ userId }: { userId: string }) {
  const { user, loading } = useUserData(userId);
  return loading ? <div>Loading...</div> :
<UserProfileDisplay user={user} />;
};
```

When components are smaller and focused, it's easier to isolate and fix issues. Debugging becomes more straightforward because you can identify the specific component responsible for the problem. Makes it easier to trace and resolve bugs.

```
// Debugging a specific component
function UserProfileDisplay({ user }: { user?: User }) {
  if (!user) return <div>No user data available</div>;
  return <div>{user.name}</div>;
};
```

Smaller components make code reviews more manageable and focused. Reviewers can concentrate on specific aspects of the code, such as data handling or UI rendering. Increases the efficiency and effectiveness of code reviews.

With well-separated components, different team members can work on different parts of the application concurrently, speeding up development. Enhances collaboration and accelerates development cycles.

Their isolate specific functionality makes it easier to write focused and targeted tests for each component. This modularity allows you to cover more scenarios with precision, reduces test complexity, and simplifies debugging when a test fails. Additionally, smaller components encourage better code organization, leading to higher test coverage and more maintainable test suites.

Smaller, focused components can lead to a more optimized and responsive user experience by efficiently managing rendering and updates. Provides a smoother and more responsive user interface.

Unique and Stable Keys

Using a unique and stable key for list items in React is essential for efficient rendering and accurate component updates. Indexes can be unreliable due to their instability in the face of list changes, leading to potential performance issues and state management problems. By adhering to this clean code principle and using unique identifiers, you ensure that React can perform its reconciliation process effectively, resulting in a smoother and more predictable user experience.

Always use a unique and stable identifier for the key prop rather than using the index of the array. Using index as the key can lead to issues if the items in array changes, as React might have trouble correctly identifying which items have changed.

Reasons for Avoiding Index as Key

Key Stability
• Index-Based Keys: When using array indexes as keys, the key value changes if the list is reordered or items are added/removed. This can lead to inefficient rendering and unexpected behavior because React relies on keys to identify items and determine which ones need to be updated.

• Unique Identifiers: Using unique identifiers (such as IDs from your data) ensures that keys remain consistent across renders, even if the list changes. This helps React accurately track and update the components.

Performance Issues
• Index-Based Keys: React may end up re-rendering more components than necessary if the list changes, because it can't accurately identify which items have changed. This can lead to performance degradation, especially in large lists.
• Unique Identifiers: Unique keys allow React to efficiently update only the items that have actually changed, leading to better performance and smoother updates.

Preservation of Component State
• Index-Based Keys: If the component has internal state or user input (like form fields), using indexes as keys can cause issues with state preservation. React may mistakenly preserve or discard state because it doesn't correctly track item identity.
• Unique Identifiers: Unique keys ensure that the component's state is preserved correctly even if the list order or length changes.

Debugging and Maintainability
• Index-Based Keys: Debugging can be more challenging when using indexes because it can be harder to track down

issues related to list reordering or item removal.

• Unique Identifiers: Using unique keys makes it clearer which item corresponds to which component, aiding in debugging and making the codebase more maintainable.

Exporting a Function As

When writing functions in TypeScript, you have the option to define and export them in different ways. Two common methods are:
• Defining the function as a "function" declaration.
• Defining the function as a "const" with an arrow function or function expression.

Function Declaration
```
export function myFunction() {
  // Function logic
}
```

Function Expression
```
export const myFunction = () => {
  // Function logic
};
```

Benefits of Using Function Declarations

Hoisting
• Function declarations are hoisted to the top of their scope, meaning they can be called before they are defined in the code. This can lead to cleaner and more intuitive code, as the function can be used before its definition.
• Function expressions are not hoisted. Attempting to call the function before its definition will result in a runtime error.

111

```
console.log(myFunction()); // Works with function
declaration, throws error with function expression
function myFunction() {
  return "Hello!";
}
const myFunction = () => {
  return "Hello!";
};
```

Readability and Clarity
• Function declarations are often easier to read and scan, particularly in large codebases. The "function" keyword clearly indicates that the code is a function definition.
• Function expressions, especially with arrow functions, can sometimes be less visually distinct in the code, potentially reducing readability.

Named Functions
• Function declarations inherently have a name, which can be beneficial for debugging. The function name will appear in stack traces, making it easier to identify where an error occurred.
• Function expressions can also have names, but this is less common in practice.

Using function declarations provides a consistent and familiar syntax, particularly for developers coming from other programming languages where functions are typically declared using similar keywords.

When to Use Function Expressions

Arrow functions capture the "this" value from their enclosing context. This behavior is particularly useful in React components and other contexts where you need to preserve the value of "this".

```
class MyClass {
  myMethod = () => {
    console.log(this); // "this" refers to the instance of MyClass
  };
}
```

Function expressions can be anonymous and assigned to variables, passed as arguments, or used as immediately invoked function expressions (IIFE).

```
const myFunction = function() {
  // Function logic
};
```

Function expressions are often used in closures, where the function needs to capture and use variables from its surrounding scope.

```
function createCounter() {
  let count = 0;
  return function() {
    return ++count;
  };
}
const counter = createCounter();
console.log(counter()); // 1
console.log(counter()); // 2
```

While both function declarations and function expressions have their uses in TypeScript, function declarations generally offer benefits in terms of hoisting, readability, and clarity. They are often preferable when defining standalone functions that do not rely on capturing the "this" value or when a named function is beneficial for debugging. Function expressions and arrow functions, on the other hand, are useful in scenarios requiring lexical scoping of "this", anonymous functions, or closures. By choosing the appropriate function definition method for the context, you can write more maintainable and understandable code.

Extracting Types, Constants, and Business Logic

Extracting Types, Constants, and Business Logic from a component offers several benefits that enhance code maintainability, readability, and testability. One effective practice is to keep the types, constants, business logic, and component's styles in the same folder as the corresponding component.

One way to manage this is by using a naming convention where types for a specific component are stored in a separate file named after the component with the suffix ".types.ts" and imported using "import type" instead of just plain "import". And by extracting constants from your components into a dedicated file with the suffix ".consts.ts". The business logic can be extracted from your components into a dedicated file with the suffix ".logic.ts" or ".utils.ts". The hooks can be extracted in a ".hooks.ts" file or in a file located in a folder "hooks" containing hooks used by the whole application.

Only the types that are used by other components or functions should be extracted into shared files. This practice keeps your codebase clean and avoids unnecessary complexity, ensuring that only relevant types are accessible across the application while keeping

115

component-specific types localized.

Styles in a React application can be considered a special case of constants because they often represent fixed values, such as colors, fonts, and layout dimensions, that can be reused throughout the application. By treating styles as constants, you can centralize and manage them in a dedicated file, promoting consistency, easy maintenance, and reusability across components. Styles for a component should be extracted into a separate ".style.ts" or ".css" file to maintain clean separation of concerns. This keeps the component file focused on logic and rendering, while the styles are managed independently.

By extracting constants, business logic, and styles into separate files, you can easily mock them during testing. This separation allows you to focus tests on components' behavior by replacing external dependencies with controlled mock data or functions, resulting in more reliable and isolated tests.

By separating types, constants, and business logic into distinct files, you enforce a clear separation of concerns. This makes the codebase easier to navigate and understand. Also it encourages modular design where each file has a single responsibility, adhering to the Single Responsibility Principle (SRP). This modularity simplifies both development and maintenance.

When types, constants, and functions are separated, updating or modifying one aspect of the code (e.g., a utility function) is easier and less likely to affect unrelated parts of the codebase. Separate files for constants and utility functions make it easier to reuse code across different parts of the application, reducing duplication.

With types, constants, and utility functions in separate files, you can write focused and targeted tests for each unit of functionality. This improves test granularity and coverage. Testing isolated logic or utilities becomes more straightforward because you can mock or stub dependencies more easily, and test each component independently of the rest of the application.

Extracting functions and logic into their own files allows you to write tests that cover all possible scenarios and edge cases for that logic. This leads to more comprehensive code coverage. When the logic is separated, maintaining and updating tests becomes simpler. You can test changes to the logic independently from changes to other parts of the application.

Example of Organizing Your React Component Files

- Component.tsx: Contains the main React component that uses the following files.
- Component.hooks.ts: Contains component's hooks of a Smart Component.
- Component.types.ts: Contains component's TypeScript types and interfaces.
- Component.consts.ts: Contains component's constants.
- Component.utils.ts: Contains business logic functions of a Smart Component.
- Component.style.ts: Contains component's style of a Dumb or Layout Component.
- __tests__/Component.test.tsx: Contains render tests for component.
- __tests__/Component.utils.test.ts: Contains unit tests for component's business logic functions.
- __mocks__/Component.tsx: Contains a mock of this component. It can be a component which renders only a div with an attribute identifying it (like data-testid="Component").
- __mocks__/Component.utils.ts: Contains mocks of the business logic functions.

Benefits for Testing and Code Coverage

By isolating functions and constants, you can write focused

tests that target specific functionality or constants without being affected by other code.

Distinct files for logic and utilities make it easier to cover all possible scenarios in tests, ensuring that edge cases and different inputs are tested.
Code coverage measures how much of your code is executed during tests. However, it generally ignores types, constants and styles, as they are not executable code but fixed values. This focus ensures that tests target the functional parts of the codebase rather than static or unchanging elements.

Using mocks for a component in tests allows you to simulate and control the behavior of dependencies, ensuring that tests are isolated and reliable. This approach enables you to test the component's functionality independently, without relying on real implementations, which leads to faster and more focused testing.

Extracting types, constants, business logic, and styles into distinct files adheres to the clean code principle of maintaining clear organization and separation of concerns. This practice not only improves code readability and maintainability but also facilitates more effective testing and comprehensive code coverage. By organizing code into manageable, focused units, you enhance the overall quality and robustness of your codebase.

Memoized Callbacks and Values in React

In React, memoization refers to optimizing the performance of your components by ensuring that functions (callbacks) and values (props) are not unnecessarily re-created on every render. This can have a significant impact on the efficiency of your application, especially in complex or frequently re-rendering components.

Memoized Callbacks

When you wrap a callback function with **useCallback**, React will return a memoized version of that function. This means that the same function reference will be used between renders, as long as the dependencies havent changed. This is particularly useful when passing callbacks to child components that are wrapped with React.memo. It prevents the child component from re-rendering unless necessary, improving performance by avoiding unnecessary renders.

```
const handleClick = useCallback(() => {
// some logic here
}, []);
```

Without useCallback, a new function reference is created on every render. If this function is passed down to child components, it can cause them to re-render unnecessarily, even if their props havent changed. This can lead to performance degradation, especially if the component tree is deep or the function is passed to multiple children.

Memoized Values

useMemo memoizes the result of a computation so that it only re-executes when its dependencies change. This means that the same computed value is returned on subsequent renders unless the dependencies are updated. Memoized values are useful when you have expensive calculations, derived data that shouldn't be recomputed on every render or data which is used as prop. By ensuring that the same reference is passed to child components, you can prevent unnecessary renders.

```
const computedValue = useMemo(() => {
  return expensiveComputation();
}, [dependency]);
```

Without useMemo, the calculation is performed on every render, and a new value reference is created each time. Passing this new reference to child components can cause them to re-render, even when the actual value hasn't changed. This can lead to inefficient rendering, as computations are repeated and unnecessary re-renders occur.

Summary of Differences

• With Memoization: Functions and values maintain their references between renders unless dependencies change. This minimizes unnecessary re-renders, making your application more efficient and performant.
• Without Memoization: New references are created on every render, which can trigger unnecessary re-renders in child components, potentially leading to performance issues.

Shadow DOM and memoization

• Shadow DOM
Encapsulates a component's styles and structure, preventing them from interfering with the rest of the page. It doesn't influence how often a component re-renders or how efficiently React handles rendering.

• Memoization
Optimizes React's rendering performance by preventing unnecessary re-renders. It ensures that functions and values maintain the same reference unless dependencies change, which is crucial for preventing performance issues in React components.

Shadow DOM and memoization serve different purposes and address different challenges in web development. The

Shadow DOM doesn't control component re-renders, so it can't replace memoization. Memoization is still necessary to manage render efficiency, even when using the Shadow DOM for encapsulation.

In essence, memoizing callbacks and values is a strategy to optimize rendering in React. While its not always necessary for every function or value, applying memoization in the right places can significantly enhance the performance of your application, especially in larger or more complex components.

State Management: React Context vs. Redux Toolkit

State management is a crucial aspect of building scalable and maintainable React applications. React provides different tools for managing state across components, with React Context and Redux Toolkit being two of the most popular. While they can both handle state management, they serve different purposes and excel in different scenarios. React Context is excellent for straightforward, localized state sharing, while Redux shines in managing complex global state with a structured approach. By leveraging Redux's powerful selectors, you can ensure that only the necessary parts of your application re-render, maintaining performance even as your state grows in complexity.

React Context

React Context is a built-in feature that allows you to share state globally across your component tree without passing props manually at every level. It's perfect for simple or small-scale state management needs where data needs to be shared among deeply nested components.

How It Works:
- Context Provider: A component that holds the state and

makes it available to other components in the tree.

• Context Consumer: Components that consume the state provided by the context.

Example of Use Cases:

• Theme Management: Sharing light and dark mode settings across your app.

• Localization: Passing down language settings without prop drilling.

• User Authentication: Managing user data and authentication status.

Limitations:

• Uncontrolled Re-renders: When the state changes, all consuming components re-render, even if only a small part of the state was updated. This can lead to performance issues if the context state is large or frequently updated.

• Limited Scope: Best suited for small-scale state management and can become cumbersome with complex state needs.

Redux Toolkit

Redux Toolkit is a predictable state container specifically designed for managing complex state across larger applications. It provides a single source of truth for the state, strict unidirectional data flow, and a consistent way to manage state updates with actions and reducers.

How It Works
- Store: Holds the entire state of the application.
- Reducers: Pure functions that determine how the state is updated based on actions.
- Actions: Plain objects that describe what should change in the state.
- Dispatch: A function used to send actions to the store.
- Selectors: Functions that extract specific slices of the state, optimizing re-renders by updating only when the selected state changes.

Example of Use Cases:
- Complex State Management: Managing complex state that needs to be accessed by many components, like a shopping cart in an e-commerce app.
- Global State: Data that needs to be available globally, such as user authentication and notifications.
- Cross-Component Communication: When multiple components need to interact with the same state.

Advantages of Redux with Selectors:
- Optimized Re-renders: Selectors can optimize component updates by ensuring that only components dependent on a particular slice of state will re-render when that specific state changes.
- Scalability: Redux's structured approach with reducers, actions, and selectors allows for easy scaling as the application grows.

• Predictable State Updates: Redux provides a predictable state update mechanism with a clear flow, making debugging easier.

Choosing Between React Context and Redux Toolkit

Use React Context if:
• Your state is simple and doesn't require complex updates.
• You are only sharing data between a few components.
• You do not need the advanced features of Redux, like middleware, dev tools, or side effects handling.

Use Redux if:
• Your application has complex, global state management needs.
• Multiple components need to access and modify the same state.
• You need features like time-travel debugging, middleware for side effects (like API calls), and consistency in state management.
• Performance Optimization: Redux selectors allow components to update only when the specific part of the state they depend on changes, avoiding unnecessary re-renders that can occur with Context.

Error Handling

Effective error handling is crucial for building robust and reliable applications. Implementing proper error handling provides numerous benefits, from improving user experience to enhancing maintainability and debugging. Here's an overview of the key benefits of error handling in these contexts:

By handling errors properly, you can ensure that users experience less disruption and receive helpful feedback when something goes wrong. Provides a fallback UI and prevents the entire application from crashing, improving user satisfaction.

```
// React component with error boundary
class ErrorBoundary extends React.Component {
  state = { hasError: false };
  static getDerivedStateFromError() {
    return { hasError: true };
  }
  componentDidCatch(error: Error, info: React.ErrorInfo) {
    console.error('Error caught by ErrorBoundary:', error, info);
  }
  render() {
    if (this.state.hasError) {
      return <h1>Something went wrong.</h1>;
    }
    return this.props.children;
  }
}
```

Proper error handling provides detailed information about errors, making it easier to diagnose and fix issues. Allows developers to understand and address errors more effectively.

```
// Async function with error handling
async function fetchData(url: string) {
  try {
    const response = await fetch(url);
    if (!response.ok) {
      throw new Error(`HTTP error! Status:
${response.status}`);
    }
    return await response.json();
  } catch (error) {
    console.error('Fetch data error:', error);
    throw error; // Re-throw for further handling
  }
};
```

Effective error handling helps prevent unexpected crashes and ensures that errors are managed in a controlled manner. Ensures that the application remains stable even when errors occur.

```
// Example of handling errors in a React component
function MyComponent() {
  const [data, setData] = React.useState<string | null>(null);
  const [error, setError] = React.useState<string | null>(null);
  React.useEffect(() => {
    fetchData('/api/data')
      .then((result) => setData(result))
      .catch((err) => setError(err.message));
  }, []);
  if (error) {
```

```
    return <div>Error: {error}</div>;
  }
  return <div>Data: {data}</div>;
};
```

Proper error handling allows you to provide informative messages to users, guiding them on how to proceed or recover from errors. Enhances the user experience by providing clear and actionable feedback.

```
// Form submission with error handling
async function handleSubmit(formData: FormData) {
  try {
    await submitForm(formData);
  } catch (error) {
    alert('Failed to submit the form. Please try again later.');
  }
};
```

By handling errors consistently, you can simplify code maintenance and avoid scattering error-handling logic throughout the codebase. Promotes cleaner code and easier updates to error-handling strategies.

```
// Custom error handling hook
function useErrorHandler() {
  const handleError = (error: Error) => {
    console.error('An error occurred:', error);
  };
  return { handleError };
};
```

Proper error handling helps prevent security vulnerabilities by ensuring that errors are managed and sensitive information is not exposed. Helps protect against information leakage and ensures that error handling does not introduce new security risks.

```
// Example of error handling with secure logging
async function fetchUserData(userId: string) {
  try {
    const response = await fetch(`/api/users/${userId}`);
    if (!response.ok) {
      throw new Error(`User not found: ${userId}`);
    }
    return await response.json();
  } catch (error) {
    // Log error securely
    console.error('Error fetching user data:', error);
    throw error;
  }
};
```

Error handling makes it easier to create test scenarios for different failure conditions and ensure that the application behaves as expected under error conditions. Ensures that the application handles errors correctly and behaves as expected in different failure scenarios.

```
// Testing error handling in React component
test('displays error message on data fetch failure', async ()
=> {
  // Mock fetch to reject promise
  global.fetch = jest.fn(() =>
    Promise.reject(new Error('Network error'))
  ) as jest.Mock;

  const { findByText } = render(<MyComponent />);
  expect(await findByText('Error: Network
error')).toBeInTheDocument();
```

```
});
```

Best Practices for Error Handling

Prefer using exceptions for error handling.

Include context information with exceptions to aid debugging.

Implement error boundaries to catch and handle errors in React components and prevent the entire app from crashing.

Provide informative and user-friendly error messages and ensure the application remains functional even when errors occur.

Define meaningful exception classes to represent different error conditions.

Use centralized logging mechanisms to capture and analyze errors for debugging and monitoring purposes.

Create and run tests for various error scenarios to ensure that error handling logic works correctly and the application behaves as expected.

Avoid exposing sensitive information in error messages and logs to prevent security vulnerabilities.

By implementing effective error handling in React, you can significantly enhance the reliability, maintainability, and user experience of your applications.

Testing

Testing is a critical practice in modern software development that ensures your application behaves as expected and helps maintain code quality over time. Testing offers a range of benefits that enhance the reliability, maintainability, and overall quality of your application.

Testing helps identify bugs and issues before they reach production. By writing tests, you can verify that your components and functions behave correctly under various conditions. Reduces the likelihood of bugs and improves the stability of your application.

```
// Unit test for a React component
test('Button component renders with correct label', () => {
  const { getByText } = render(<Button label="Click Me"
onClick={() => {}} />);
  expect(getByText('Click Me')).toBeInTheDocument();
});
```

Tests ensure that the code meets its functional requirements and behaves as expected. This validation helps maintain high code quality and correctness. Validates that the code produces the correct results, improving overall code quality.

```
// Testing a utility function
test('calculateTotal calculates the total correctly', () => {
  const result = calculateTotal([10, 20, 30]);
```

```
  expect(result).toBe(60);
});
```

With a robust test suite, you can confidently refactor code knowing that existing functionality will be preserved. Tests act as a safety net, ensuring that changes do not break existing features. Facilitates code improvements and structural changes without introducing new bugs.

// Refactoring a component and running tests to ensure nothing is broken

Tests serve as living documentation that describes how the components and functions should behave. This documentation is always up-to-date with the code. Provides clear and current information about the code's behavior, helping new developers understand the application.

// Test cases describe the expected behavior of a component or function

Automated tests give developers confidence that their changes will not negatively impact the existing functionality of the application. This confidence speeds up the development process and reduces the likelihood of introducing errors. Enhances developer confidence and accelerates the development workflow.

// Running tests after a code change to ensure everything still works

Tests provide immediate feedback during development, allowing developers to catch issues early and iterate quickly. Improves the development process by catching issues sooner.

// Running tests in the development process to catch errors as they occur

When tests fail, they pinpoint the location and nature of issues, making debugging more efficient and straightforward. Streamlines the debugging process and reduces time spent identifying issues.

// Test failures provide information about what went wrong and where

Writing tests encourages developers to write modular and testable code. This leads to better separation of concerns and a cleaner architecture. Promotes a well-structured and maintainable codebase.

// Testing a small, isolated component encourages modular design

Integration with CI/CD pipelines allows automated tests to run on every code change, ensuring that new code does not break the application. Ensures consistent quality and reliability throughout the development process.

// Integrating tests into a CI/CD pipeline for automatic execution

Tests help team members understand the expected behavior of components and functions, fostering better collaboration and alignment within the team. Facilitates better communication and collaboration among developers.

// Using tests as a reference for component behavior during team discussions

Types of Testing in TypeScript and React

● Unit Testing
Tests individual functions or components in isolation. Validates the functionality of small units of code.

Jest, React Testing Library

● Integration Testing
Tests interactions between components or systems to ensure they work together correctly. Ensures that different parts of the application work together as expected.

Jest, React Testing Library

● End-to-End Testing
Tests the entire application flow from the user's perspective to ensure it behaves as intended. Validates the complete user experience and application functionality.

Cypress, Selenium, Playwright

• Snapshot Testing

Captures the rendered output of components and compares it to previous versions to detect unintended changes. Ensures that UI changes are intentional and expected.

Jest

Best Practices for Testing

Unit tests should run quickly.

Tests should not depend on each other.

Tests should produce the same results every time.

Tests should have a clear pass or fail result.

Ensure tests clearly describe the expected behavior or what it is verifying. Use meaningful test names. This makes it easier to understand the purpose of the test at a glance. For example, instead of "test('works correctly')", use "test('should render the header with the correct title')".

Write tests that focus on small, isolated units of your code, such as individual functions or components. Make them independent and to do not rely on the state or behavior of other tests. This ensures that tests are easier to write, understand, and maintain. Each test should cover a unique aspect of the functionality, avoiding redundancy.

In some cases, isolated tests might be difficult to implement when checking preconditions is complex. In these situations, it can be acceptable for a test to assume that a previous test successfully verified the preconditions. This approach reduces redundancy and simplifies the testing process, but should be used cautiously to avoid introducing dependencies between tests.

For React components, use snapshot testing to capture and compare the rendered output. This helps ensure that your UI remains consistent over time. Only update snapshots when you are sure that the changes are intentional and correct.

Use integration tests to verify how different parts of your application work together, such as how components interact with state management or APIs. Ensure that your tests simulate real-world scenarios that a user might encounter.

Ensure your tests cover edge cases, such as invalid inputs or unexpected user behavior, to ensure the robustness of your code. Test how your code handles errors and exceptions, ensuring that it behaves gracefully under adverse conditions.

Prioritize writing tests for the most critical and complex parts of your application where bugs would have the most impact. If you're working with a legacy codebase or a large application, start by covering the most crucial areas and expand test coverage over time.

When testing a component or function that relies on external dependencies (like APIs, databases, or other components), use mocks to isolate the unit under test. Tools like Jest provide easy-to-use mocking capabilities that help simulate different scenarios without relying on actual implementations.

If a test is particularly complex or not immediately obvious, add comments to explain its purpose and logic. Document your overall test strategy, including what types of tests are used (unit, integration, end-to-end), where they are located, and how they should be run.

Use variables and setup functions to avoid hard-coding data in your tests, making them easier to maintain and update. When refactoring code, ensure that tests are updated to reflect the changes. This keeps your tests relevant and accurate.

Use tools like Jest's coverage reports to measure how much of your code is covered by tests. Aim for high coverage but focus on covering critical and complex parts of the code. Some parts of the code, like constants or simple getter methods, may not need to be tested extensively.

Run tests frequently during development, not just before merging or releasing. Continuous testing helps catch issues early. Implement continuous integration/continuous deployment (CI/CD) pipelines that automatically run tests on each commit or pull request, ensuring that your code remains stable.

By incorporating testing practices in your TypeScript projects, you can ensure that your application is reliable, maintainable, and performs as expected. This leads to a higher-quality product, improved developer experience, and enhanced confidence in the codebase.

Test Driven Development (TDD)

Test Driven Development (TDD) is a software development process where developers write tests for a new feature before writing the actual code to implement that feature. The cycle of TDD consists of three main steps, often referred to as "Red-Green-Refactor":

- Red

Write a test for a new feature or functionality. At this point, the test should fail because the feature hasn't been implemented yet.

- Green

Write the minimum amount of code necessary to make the test pass. This code is often simple and not yet optimized.

- Refactor

Clean up the code while ensuring that all tests still pass. Refactoring helps improve the code's structure and readability without changing its behavior.

Setting Up the Environment

Install Required Packages
- React Testing Library: A popular library for testing React components.

- Jest: A testing framework often used with React.
- TypeScript: To ensure type safety and better development experience.

```
npm install --save-dev jest @testing-library/react @testing-library/jest-dom typescript ts-jest
```

Configure Jest for TypeScript

Create a "jest.config.js" file to configure Jest with TypeScript.

```
module.exports = {
  preset: 'ts-jest',
  testEnvironment: 'jsdom',
  moduleFileExtensions: ['ts', 'tsx'],
  transform: {
    '^.+\\.(ts|tsx)$': 'ts-jest',
  },
  testMatch: ['**/?(*.)+(test).(ts|tsx)'],
};
```

Structure of the Test Files

React Components

```
describe('pathTo/ComponentFilename.tsx', () => {
  test('name of the test', () => {
    render(<Component ... />);

    ...
    expect(...).to...(...);
  });
  // add more tests till you cover all use cases or props combinations
  });
```

Business Logic

```
describe('pathTo/ComponentFilename.utils.ts', () => {
  describe('functionName', () => {
    test('name of the test', () => {
      const result = functionName(...);

      ...
      expect(result).toEqual(...);
    });
    // add more tests till you cover all use cases or arguments
combinations
  });
  // add tests for all other exported business logic functions
});
```

Utility Functions

```
describe('pathTo/UtilityFilename.ts', () => {
  describe('functionName', () => {
    test('name of the test', () => {
      const result = functionName(...);

      ...
      expect(result).toEqual(...);
    });
    // add more tests till you cover all use cases or arguments
combinations
  });
  // add tests for all other exported business logic functions
});
```

Writing Tests Before Code

• Red Phase: Write All Meaningfull Tests
Start by writing all the tests - postive and negative - for a
new feature, component or function before implementing

the actual code. In this way you have a chance to think over all possible use cases without being biased by the implementation. Also gives you a chance to understand or clarify the requirements, and obtain any missing information.

```
// __tests__/Button.test.tsx
import { render, screen } from '@testing-library/react';
import '@testing-library/jest-dom/extend-expect';
import Button from '../components/Button';
describe('Button.tsx', () => {
  test('renders a button with the correct label', () => {
    render(<Button label="Click Me" />);
    const buttonElement = screen.getByText(/Click Me/i);
    expect(buttonElement).toBeInTheDocument();
  });
});
```

• Green Phase: Write the Minimum Code to Pass the Test

Implement the simplest possible solution to make the test pass.

```
// components/Button.tsx
type ButtonProps = {
  label: string;
};
export function Button({ label }: ButtonProps) {
  return <button>{label}</button>;
};
```

• Refactor Phase: Improve the Code While Keeping Tests Passing

Refactor the code for better readability, maintainability,

and performance. Ensure all tests still pass after refactoring.

```
// components/Button.tsx (Refactored)
import { memo } from 'react';
type ButtonProps = {
  label: string;
};
export const Button: React.FC<ButtonProps> = memo(({
label }) => {
  return <button>{label}</button>;
});
```

Benefits of TDD

TypeScript provides type checking at compile time, reducing runtime errors and improving the reliability of the codebase.

Writing tests first helps catch bugs early in the development process.

TDD encourages writing smaller, more focused functions and components, leading to better code design.

Tests serve as a form of documentation, explaining what the code is supposed to do.

With a robust suite of tests, developers can refactor code with confidence, knowing that tests will catch any regressions.

Example of TDD in Action

- Red Phase

Write a test for a new feature that checks if a button is disabled when a "disabled" prop is passed.

```
// __tests__/Button.test.tsx
test('renders a disabled button when the disabled prop is
true', () => {
  render(<Button label="Click Me" disabled={true} />);
  const buttonElement = screen.getByText(/Click Me/i);
  expect(buttonElement).toBeDisabled();
});
```

- Green Phase

Implement the feature to pass the test.

```
// components/Button.tsx
type ButtonProps = {
  label: string;
  disabled?: boolean;
};
function Button({ label, disabled = false }: ButtonProps) {
  return <button disabled={disabled}>{label}</button>;
};
```

- Refactor Phase

Ensure the code is clean and all tests pass.

```
// components/Button.tsx (Refactored)
type ButtonProps = {
  label: string;
  disabled?: boolean;
};
```

```
const Button: React.FC<ButtonProps> = memo(({ label,
disabled = false }) => {
  return <button disabled={disabled}>{label}</button>;
});
```

Start with Test-Driven Development (TDD) today. Begin by writing tests before you write the actual code. This approach ensures that your code meets the requirements and that edge cases are considered from the start. TDD helps you focus on the requirements of your code, ensuring that each function or component does exactly what it's supposed to do.

By following TDD principles, developers can build TypeScript and React applications that are reliable, maintainable, easy to understand, and have effective, reliable tests.

Code Reviews

Code Reviews involve systematically examining code written by team members to ensure it meets the project's standards and quality requirements. They are a collaborative process that enhances code quality and promotes knowledge sharing.

Reviews help identify bugs and issues early, reducing the likelihood of defects reaching production. Ensures that code meets quality standards and reduces errors.

```
// Review might catch an incorrect type assignment
const user: string = 123; // TypeScript error caught during
code review
```

Code reviews provide an opportunity for team members to learn from each other, sharing best practices and new techniques. Promotes team growth and improves overall code practices.

```
// A reviewer suggests using a hook for state
management instead of class components
```

Reviews help ensure that code adheres to the team's coding standards and style guidelines. Maintains a consistent code style across the codebase.

```
// Enforcing consistent use of TypeScript TYPEs for props
interface ButtonProps { // It shhould be a type
  label: string;
```

```
  onClick: () => void;
}
```

Feedback from reviews can improve code readability by suggesting better naming conventions and structuring. Makes the code easier to understand and maintain.

```
// Renaming ambiguous variable names
const userProfileData = userProfile; // Reviewer suggests
clearer name
```

Reviews encourage communication and collaboration among team members, fostering a more cohesive development environment. Strengthens team dynamics and ensures aligned understanding of code.

```
// Discussing architectural decisions and approaches
during the review
```

Reviews create a historical record of changes and discussions, which can be useful for understanding why certain decisions were made. Provides context and rationale for future reference.

```
// Documenting the reason for a refactor in the review
comments
```

Refactoring

Refactoring involves restructuring existing code without changing its external behavior to improve its internal structure, readability, and performance. It aims to make the codebase more efficient and maintainable.

Refactoring makes code easier to understand and modify by removing redundancies and improving structure. Facilitates easier updates and debugging.

```
// Refactoring a large component into smaller, reusable
components
function UserProfile({ user }: UserProfileProps) { /*...*/ };
function UserPosts({ posts }: UserPostsProps) { /*...*/ };
```

Refactoring can lead to performance improvements by optimizing algorithms and reducing unnecessary computations. Enhances the efficiency and responsiveness of the application.

```
// Optimizing a rendering function to avoid unnecessary
re-renders
const UserList: FC<{ users: User[] }> = memo(({ users }) => {
  return <ul>{users.map(user => <li
key={user.id}>{user.name}</li>)}</ul>;
});
```

Refactoring can make code more modular and testable by breaking it into smaller, more focused units. Simplifies the process of writing and maintaining tests.

```
// Refactoring a complex function into smaller, testable
functions
function calculateDiscount(price: number, discount:
number): number { /*...*/ };
function applyTax(price: number, taxRate: number):
number { /*...*/ };
```

Regular refactoring helps manage technical debt by addressing issues and improving code quality over time. Keeps the codebase healthy and adaptable to future changes.

```
// Addressing legacy code issues and improving design
patterns
```

Refactoring improves the organization of code, making it more logical and easier to navigate. Enhances the clarity and organization of the codebase.

```
// Reorganizing project files and components
src/
  components/
    Button.tsx
    UserProfile.tsx
  hooks/
    useForm.ts
```

A well-structured codebase allows for faster feature development and easier bug fixes. Accelerates the development process and reduces time to market.

```
// Adding new features to a well-organized codebase
with minimal disruption
```

Best Practices for Code Reviews and Refactoring

Conduct code reviews regularly to maintain high code quality and foster team collaboration.

Adhere to coding standards and best practices to ensure consistency and readability in the codebase.

Provide constructive and respectful feedback during code reviews to promote learning and improvement.

Implement refactoring in small, manageable increments to minimize risks and disruptions.

Document reasons for refactoring and decisions made during code reviews to provide context for future reference.

Utilize automated code review and refactoring tools to streamline the process and catch common issues.

By integrating code reviews and refactoring practices into your development workflow, you can enhance the quality, maintainability, and performance of your codebase, leading to more efficient and reliable applications.

Demo App

We will create a Web Application called "Data Display App".
It is a React application built with TypeScript that
showcases a modular and reusable approach to displaying
data fetched from an API. The app leverages React Router
to read an ID from the URL, fetches data based on this ID,
and dynamically renders the data in a structured layout.

Key Features

Uses React Router to extract parameters from the URL for
dynamic data fetching.

Fetches data from an API endpoint based on the URL
parameter.

Implements a GenericList component to render lists of
items, promoting code reuse.

Utilizes a LayoutComponent to organize and display
names and tags fetched from the API.

Ensures type safety and improved developer experience
with TypeScript.

Usage

Navigate to a route like /data/:id where :id is a dynamic parameter used to fetch specific data.

The app fetches a JSON array of objects, each containing name and tag fields, from the endpoint /api/nameTags/:id.

Names and tags are extracted from the fetched data and displayed using the GenericList component within a structured layout.

Visiting `/nameTags/123` we fetch data like:
```
[
  { "name": "Alice", "tag": "Developer" },
  { "name": "Bob", "tag": "Designer" },
  { "name": "Charlie", "tag": "Manager" }
]
```

This data is then displayed in separate lists for names and tags.

Workflow

First, we demonstrate how a component is often written in a single function, as typically seen in real projects. This approach might work, but it can lead to a cluttered and difficult-to-maintain codebase. Then, we break down the component into smaller, more focused functions,

155

explaining a better way to create it. This improved approach brings numerous benefits, such as increased readability, easier testing, and better reusability, ultimately leading to cleaner, more maintainable code.

```
// src/MainComponent.tsx
// This is a all-in-one component

import { useEffect, useState } from 'react';
import { useParams } from 'react-router-dom';
import { GenericList } from './GenericList';
import { LayoutComponents } from './LayoutComponents';

type NameTagList = Array<NameTag>;
type NameTag = {
 name: string;
 tag: string;
};

type RouteParams = {
 id: string;
};

export function MainComponent() {
 const { id } = useParams<RouteParams>();
 const [names, setNames] = useState<string[]>([]);
 const [tags, setTags] = useState<string[]>([]);

 useEffect(() => {
  const fetchData = async () => {
   try {
    const response = await fetch(`/api/nameTags/${id}`);
    const data: NameTagList = await response.json();
    setNames(getNames(data));
    setTags(getTags(data));
   } catch {
    showError('Error');
   }
```

```tsx
    };
    fetchData();
  }, [id]);

  return (
    <LayoutComponents
      names={<GenericList title="Names" items={names} />}
      tags={<GenericList title="Tags" items={tags} />}
    />
  );
}

function getNames(list: NameTagList): Array<string> {
  const names = list.map(({ name }) => name);
  names.sort();
  return names;
}

function getTags(list: NameTagList): Array<string> {
  const tags = list.map(({ tag }) => tag);
  tags.sort();
  return tags.filter((tag, index, tagList) => index ===
tagList.indexOf(tag));
}

function showError(message: string): void {
  console.error(message);
}
```

```
// src/LayoutComponents.tsx
// It is a Dumb Component responsible only with layouting of
two components

import { ReactNode } from 'react';
import { style } from './LayoutComponents.style';

type Props = {
  names: ReactNode;
  tags: ReactNode;
};

export function LayoutComponents({ names, tags }: Props) {
  return (
    <div style={style}>
     {names}
     {tags}
    </div>
  );
}

// src/LayoutComponents.style.ts
// We need to change only this file for a different layouting

import { CSSProperties } from 'react';

export const style: CSSProperties = {
  display: 'flex',
  gap: 20,
};
```

```tsx
// src/GenericList.tsx
type Props<T> = {
  items: T[];
  title: string;
};

export function GenericList<T extends string>({ items, title }:
Props<T>) {
  return (
    <div>
      <h1>{title}</h1>
      <ul>
       {items.map((item, index) => (
         <li key={index}>{item}</li>
        ))}
      </ul>
    </div>
  );
}
```

The problems

The provided code, while functional, violates several coding principles presented in this book, leading to potential issues in maintainability, readability, and testing. Here is a breakdown of the problems:

● Single Responsibility Principle (SRP) Violation:
The MainComponent handles multiple responsibilities: fetching data, transforming data, handling errors, and rendering the UI. We can separate these concerns into distinct components or utility functions. For example, data fetching could be moved to a custom hook, and data transformation functions could be moved to a utility file.

● Large Component (Lack of Separation of Concerns)
The MainComponent is an "all-in-one" component, making it large and difficult to understand at a glance. We should break down the component into smaller, more focused components. Each component should handle a specific part of the logic, such as data fetching, data transformation, and rendering.

● Functions Not Grouped by Usage
The helper functions are defined within the same file but

outside the component, disrupting the flow of reading the component. We need to extract these helper functions to a separate utility file, and only keep the code directly related to rendering within the component file. This makes the component easier to navigate and reduces cognitive load.

• Unnecessary Inline Error Handling

The showError function is defined within the same file but could be standardized across the application. Lets extract error handling into a shared utility or error handling service that can be reused across the application, enhancing consistency and reducing redundancy.

• Lack of Type Separation

The types are defined within the component file, which clutters the file and mixes concerns. We should extract the types used also in other places into a separate types file. This keeps the component file focused on the logic and UI, improving clarity and making it easier to manage types.

• Lack of Code Reusability

The logic for extracting names and tags is tightly coupled with the component, making it harder to reuse. The logic should be extracted into separate functions or a custom hook that can be reused by other components if needed.

● Error Prone with Larger Codebase

As the codebase grows, maintaining this component will become increasingly difficult due to its size and mixed responsibilities. By modularizing the component into smaller parts, each part can be maintained, tested, and refactored independently, reducing the risk of introducing bugs.

● Testing Complexity

The MainComponent in its current form is harder to test because it combines multiple concerns into a single function. By breaking the component into smaller, more focused components and functions makes unit testing easier and more effective. Each piece of logic can be tested in isolation, improving test coverage and making it easier to identify and fix bugs.

● Implicit Function Ordering

Helper functions are defined in an order that does not follow their usage in the code. The functions should be organized in the order they are used, improving the logical flow and making the code easier to follow.

Lets address these issues, by creating a cleaner, more maintainable, and testable codebase. The goal is to write code that not only works but is also easy to understand, modify, and extend over time.

```tsx
// src/MainComponent.tsx
// This is the component respecting more the Clean Code
principles

import { useParams } from 'react-router-dom';
import { GenericList } from './GenericList';
import { LayoutComponents } from './LayoutComponents';
import { useFetchData } from './MainComponent.hooks';

type RouteParams = {
  id: string;
};

export function MainComponent() {
  const { id } = useParams<RouteParams>();
  const { names, tags } = useFetchData(id);
  return (
    <LayoutComponents
      names={<GenericList title="Names" items={names} />}
      tags={<GenericList title="Tags" items={tags} />}
    />
  );
}
```

```
// src/MainComponent.types.ts
export type NameTagList = Array<NameTag>;

type NameTag = {
  name: string;
  tag: string;
};

// src/MainComponent.hooks.ts
import { useState, useEffect, useMemo } from 'react';
import { NameTagList } from './MainComponent.types';
import { getNames, getTags, showError } from
'./MainComponent.utils';

export function useFetchData(id?: string) {
  const [names, setNames] = useState<string[]>([]);
  const [tags, setTags] = useState<string[]>([]);

  useEffect(() => {
   if (!id) {
    return;
   }

   const fetchData = async () => {
    try {
     const response = await fetch(`/api/nameTags/${id}`);
     const data: NameTagList = await response.json();
     setNames(getNames(data));
     setTags(getTags(data));
    } catch {
     showError('Error');
    }
   };
```

```
    fetchData();
  }, [id]);

  return useMemo(() => ({ names, tags }), [names, tags]);
}

// src/MainComponent.utils.ts
import { NameTagList } from './MainComponent.types';

export function getNames(list: NameTagList): Array<string> {
  const names = list.map(({ name }) => name);
  names.sort();
  return names;
}

export function getTags(list: NameTagList): Array<string> {
  const tags = list.map(({ tag }) => tag);
  tags.sort();
  return tags.filter((tag, index, tagList) => index ===
tagList.indexOf(tag));
}

export function showError(message: string): void {
  console.error(message);
}
```

Mocking

Now, we'll create mocks for these components to simulate their behavior in a controlled environment. Mocks allow us to isolate and test each component without relying on external dependencies or complex setups. This approach helps ensure our tests are focused, reliable, and easier to maintain, ultimately leading to higher-quality code.

Mocked files

```tsx
// src/__mocks__/MainComponent.tsx
export function MainComponent() {
  return <div id="MainComponent" />;
}
```

```ts
// src/__mocks__/MainComponent.utils.ts
import { NameTagList } from '../MainComponent.types';

export function getNames(list: NameTagList): Array<string> {
  return ['mock-name'];
}

export function getTags(list: NameTagList): Array<string> {
  return ['mock-tag'];
}

export function showError(message: string): void {}
```

```tsx
// src/__mocks__/LayoutComponents.tsx
import { LayoutComponents as LayoutComponentsImpl }
from '../LayoutComponents';

export function LayoutComponents({ names, tags }:
Parameters<typeof LayoutComponentsImpl>[0]) {
  return (
    <div>
      {names && <div data-testid="names-placeholder" />}
      {tags && <div data-testid="tags-placeholder" />}
    </div>
  );
}
```

```tsx
// src/__mocks__/GenericList.tsx
```

```
import { GenericList as GenericListImpl } from '../GenericList';

export function GenericList({ items, title }: Parameters<typeof
GenericListImpl>[0]) {
  return (
    <div data-testid="GenericList">
     <div data-testid="title">{title}</div>
     <div data-testid="items-count">{items.length}</div>
    </div>
  );
}
```

Testing

We'll write tests for MainComponent in different ways, tests that mock different components or the business logic of components. By using mocks, we can isolate the component or function under test, simulating the behavior of its dependencies. This approach allows us to focus on the component's internal logic without worrying about the complexity or variability of its external interactions. Mocking helps create precise, targeted tests that verify the component's behavior in various scenarios, ensuring it performs as expected in the broader application.

When writing tests, it's crucial to be mindful of what is being tested and what isn't, ensuring comprehensive coverage. Additionally, review the comments at the beginning of example test files, as they provide additional information.

Don't forget to mock the API calls or responses in the following tests. The mock implementations themselves are omitted from the test cases for clarity.

```
// src/__tests__/MainComponent.test.tsx
// We do not mock anything.
// Problem: if there is a deep component composition then we
test a lot of components and business logic with one test. But
also much of the code can remain untested. Tests for these
child components will re-test what was already tested with
this test.

import { render, screen } from '@testing-library/react';
import { MainComponent } from '../MainComponent';
import { act } from 'react';

describe('MainComponent.tsx', () => {
  test('it render both lists', () => {
    act(() => {
      render(<MainComponent />);
    });
    expect(screen.getByRole('heading', { name: 'Names'
})).toBeInTheDocument();
    expect(screen.getByRole('heading', { name: 'Tags'
})).toBeInTheDocument();
  });
});
```

```
// src/__tests__/MainComponent.test.tsx
// We mock the layout component (directly in test file).
// Problem: we do not know if the layout component receives
the expected props, but only that it is rendered.

import { render, screen } from '@testing-library/react';
import { MainComponent } from '../MainComponent';
import { act } from 'react';

describe('MainComponent.tsx', () => {
  test('it render the layout', () => {
    act(() => {
      render(<MainComponent />);
    });
    expect(screen.getByTestId('LayoutComponents')).toBeInTh
eDocument();
  });
});

jest.mock('../LayoutComponents', () => ({
  __esModule: true,
  LayoutComponents: () => <div data-
testid="LayoutComponents" />,
}));
```

```
// src/__tests__/MainComponent.test.tsx
// We mock the layout component (directly in test file).
// Problem: it checks if the layout component receives the
expected props, but not their values.

import { render, screen } from '@testing-library/react';
import { MainComponent } from '../MainComponent';
import { act } from 'react';
import { LayoutComponents } from '../LayoutComponents';

describe('MainComponent.tsx', () => {
  test('it render the two lists', () => {
    act(() => {
      render(<MainComponent />);
    });
    expect(screen.getByTestId('Names')).toBeInTheDocument(
);
    expect(screen.getByTestId('Tags')).toBeInTheDocument();
  });
});

jest.mock('../LayoutComponents', () => ({
  __esModule: true,
  LayoutComponents: ({ names, tags }: Parameters<typeof
LayoutComponents>[0]) => (
    <div>
    {names && <div data-testid="Names" />}
    {tags && <div data-testid="Tags" />}
    </div>
  ),
}));
```

```
// src/__tests__/MainComponent.test.tsx
// We mock the layout component using manual mocks.
// Problem: depending how the component is mocked, some
aspects can remain untested (like props are received or
correct).

import { render, screen } from '@testing-library/react';
import { act } from 'react';
import { MainComponent } from '../MainComponent';

describe('MainComponent.tsx', () => {
  test('it render the placeholders for the two lists', () => {
    act(() => {
      render(<MainComponent />);
    });
    expect(screen.getByTestId('names-
placeholder')).toBeInTheDocument();
    expect(screen.getByTestId('tags-
placeholder')).toBeInTheDocument();
  });
});

jest.mock('../LayoutComponents');
```

```
// src/__tests__/MainComponent.test.tsx
// We mock the generic list component using manual
mocks.
// Problem: our test is dependent of the implementation of
MainComponent.

import { render, screen, waitFor, within } from '@testing-
library/react';
import { act } from 'react';
import { MainComponent } from '../MainComponent';

describe('MainComponent.tsx', () => {
  test('it render the placeholders for the two lists', async () => {
    act(() => {
      render(<MainComponent />);
    });
    expect(screen.getByText('Names')).toBeInTheDocument();
    expect(screen.getByText('Tags')).toBeInTheDocument();
    expect(screen.getAllByTestId('items-
count')).toHaveLength(2);
    await waitFor(() => {
      expect(
        within(screen.getAllByTestId('items-
count')[0]).getByText('3')
      ).toBeInTheDocument();
    });
    expect(
      within(screen.getAllByTestId('items-
count')[1]).getByText('2')
    ).toBeInTheDocument();
  });
});

jest.mock('../GenericList');
```

```tsx
// src/__tests__/MainComponent.test.tsx
// We mock the business logic of the component using
manual mocks.
// Problem: our test is dependent of the mocking of
MainComponent's business logic functions.

import { render, screen, waitFor } from '@testing-
library/react';
import { act } from 'react';
import { MainComponent } from '../MainComponent';

describe('MainComponent.tsx', () => {
  test('it render the mocks of the two lists', async () => {
    act(() => {
      render(<MainComponent />);
    });
    expect(screen.getByText('Names')).toBeInTheDocument();
    expect(screen.getByText('Tags')).toBeInTheDocument();
    await waitFor(() => {
      expect(screen.getByText('mock-
name')).toBeInTheDocument();
    });
    expect(screen.getByText('mock-
tag')).toBeInTheDocument();
  });
});

jest.mock('../MainComponent.utils');
```

```ts
// src/__tests__/MainComponent.utils.test.ts
// We can test effectively the business logic of a component.

import { mockNameTagList } from '../api/nameTags.mock';
import { getNames, getTags, showError } from
'../MainComponent.utils';

describe('MainComponent.utils.ts', () => {
  describe('getNames', () => {
    test('it returns the list sorted', () => {
      const res = getNames(mockNameTagList);
      expect(res).toEqual(['Alice', 'Bob', 'Charlie']);
    });
    // Define more tests
  });

  describe('getTags', () => {
    test('it returns the list of unique sorted tags', () => {
      const res = getTags(mockNameTagList);
      expect(res).toEqual(['Designer', 'Developer']);
    });
    // Define more tests
  });

  describe('showError', () => {
    test('it displays the error', () => {
      const mockConsoleError = jest.fn();
      console.error = mockConsoleError;
      showError('Error message');
      expect(mockConsoleError).toHaveBeenCalledWith('Error
message');
    });
  });
});
```

Writing tests for React components presents several challenges, including:

Ensuring that a component correctly renders all its child components can be challenging, especially when the child components themselves are complex or have their own dependencies. Tests need to verify that the entire component tree behaves as expected, which may require setting up mocks or stubs for child components.

Modifications to a component can unintentionally break tests for parent components. For instance, if a child component's interface changes or its behavior is altered, it might affect how the parent component renders or interacts with it, leading to test failures. This interdependency means that changes in one part of the component tree may necessitate updates to multiple tests.

React components often interact with various props, states, and contexts, making it difficult to simulate and test all possible scenarios. Ensuring that all interactions are properly tested requires careful setup and consideration of different edge cases.

Components that rely on asynchronous operations, such

as data fetching, introduce additional complexity. Tests need to handle and assert the correct behavior of components both before and after asynchronous operations complete, often requiring the use of async utilities or mocks.

While snapshot testing can help catch unexpected changes in the rendered output, it may not always capture the nuances of component behavior or interactions. Snapshots need to be carefully managed to ensure they provide meaningful validation without becoming overly brittle.

Addressing these challenges involves thorough planning and strategic testing practices, including component isolation, using appropriate mocking and stubbing techniques, and maintaining up-to-date test cases as components evolve.

Why are all types for components' props are called Props instead of ComponentNameProps?

As long as these props are not exported, the name Props is clear and meaningful enough. In case it was exported, either it was named appropriately or exported with an appropriate name. Also it respects the Consistent Naming Patterns - all props have the same type name - and Use Searchable Names - searching for the whole word Props will find all defined props in the project.

Why there is an "await waitFor" for a value but not for one coming together with the first one?

As we know that there will be more values rendered with delay but together, we want to wait for one of them to be displayed and then test that also the rest of them are present. By using "await waitFor" or "findBy" for the other assertions, we cannot know if they were displayed at once or with some delay between them.

Crafting Better Code

As you reach the end of this book, I want to take a moment to encourage you on your journey toward becoming a more effective and thoughtful developer. Writing clean, maintainable code is not just a technical skill - it's a commitment to quality, clarity, and craftsmanship. The guidelines and principles you've encountered in these pages are drawn from over 25 years of experience in software development and more than a decade working with React and TypeScript. They are tried, tested, and proven to lead to better code.

But remember, the pursuit of clean code is an ongoing process. It's about continually refining your practices, learning from every project, and embracing the mindset of a craftsman who takes pride in their work. Each line of code you write is an opportunity to apply the principles of clean code, making your software not only functionally correct but also elegant, readable, and easy to maintain.

As you apply the guidelines from this book, you'll find that your code becomes easier to understand, your projects become more scalable, and your development process becomes more efficient. By embracing these practices, you're not just improving your own work; you're contributing to a culture of excellence within your teams and the broader development community.

Keep pushing yourself to write better code. Stay curious, keep learning, and always strive to make your code cleaner and more expressive. The journey of a developer is one of constant growth, and with the principles of clean code as your guide, you are well on your way to becoming a true software craftsman.

Thank you for choosing to embark on this journey with "Coding Guidelines for React with TypeScript." The tools and practices you've learned here are powerful, but it's your dedication and passion that will ultimately drive the quality of the code you produce. Here's to creating better code - code that not only works but stands the test of time.

Iulian Radu